CONTROVERSY WITH THE INTERNATIONAL BANKERS

by Minister Louis Farrakhan

National Representative of
The Most Honourable Elijah Muhammad

HAKIKI PUBLISHING LONDON

FIRST EDITION 1996

Edited By	Olusola Odesanya X, Derek X.
Transcribed By	Olusola Odesanya X, Derek X, Tina X.
Proof Read By	Sonia X
Cover Design By	Hakiki

Copyright © Minister Louis Farrakhan Muhammad

Printed by: Lasun Graphics
Published by: Hakiki Publishing

ISBN 1 900903 900 2

'Accept your own, and be yourself'
Master W. Fard Muhammad

Why this book was written

In July of 1930, Allah (God) appeared in the person of Master W. Fard Muhammad; the long-awaited 'Messiah' of the Christians and the "Mahdi" of the Muslims. He travelled into the wilderness of North America by Himself to set free, and declare the Independence of the Black man and woman, who had been stolen from Africa in the 16th century. His aim was to search amongst the seventeen million Black people for One, whom the scriptures called Elijah, whose mission was, "to turn the hearts of the children back to the Father, and the heart of the Father back to the children," thus establishing the Nation of Islam in the West.

In August 1930, in Detroit Michigan, The Honourable Elijah Muhammad known then as Elijah Poole, intrigued by Master Fard Muhammad attended a meeting where He was teaching. During the meeting Elijah understood exactly what Master Fard Muhammad was teaching. They soon began spending a lot of time together and in 1931, Master Fard Muhammad began teaching Elijah and training him for his mission. In 1934, Elijah (now known as Elijah Karem) became the First Minister of Islam.

Elijah worked hard to establish temples and teach Islam, but he was met with obstacles. Jealousy and envy of Elijah and a misconception of what his role was to be by others, caused Elijah to flee for his life and run for seven years. He carried within him the plan for the birth of a new nation for the oppressed slaves and if he didn't run, this concept of true freedom may never have reached the ears of the masses of Black people.

While running, Elijah taught Islam and at that point in time, the government wanted Elijah silenced for they didn't want a man to tell thousands of Black people that they were somebody and they "CAN ACCOMPLISH WHAT THEY WILL."

In the 1940's, when the masses of Blacks began listening and responding to the voice of Elijah, the American government stepped in (in 1942) and jailed him under the pretence of being a draft dodger (although he was over the age of 45 and the draft only covers ages 18 to 45). When Elijah left jail, almost everything built and almost everyone taught in the religion of Islam was gone and disbanded. He began to rebuild from the remains of the Nation of Islam.

During the early 1960's, Elijah Muhammad became known as The Honourable Elijah Muhammad and was well on the way to establishing governmental order for Black people. He always showed tremendous love for the Blackman and everything he did was to better the condition of the Black community.

In 1974, The Most Honourable Elijah Muhammad completed a 40-year period (1934-1974). The year 1934, represents the time in which he was left on his own by Master Fard Muhammad. The completion of this period climaxed a historic Saviour's Day address when he spoke on 'The Black God.'

In 1974, The Most Honourable Elijah Muhammad departed, and left in our midst the Honourable Minister Louis Farrakhan, whom he spoke of in these words "Wherever you see him, look at him, wherever he asks to stay away from stay away, and wherever he asks you to go, go."

Since 1977, Minister Farrakhan has continued the work of, The Most Honorable Elijah Muhammad, spreading his teachings to the four corners of the globe, sharing the knowledge, wisdom and understanding brought to us by Master Fard Muhammad.

We are compelled to continue the great work of this Mighty Servant of Allah, by disseminating the Teachings of The Most Honorable Elijah Muhammad, by representing the myriad of lectures given by his National Representative, Minister Louis Farrakhan, into written form.

These Teachings are profound in their effect and in their ability to transform human life, helping in the resurrection of a people considered nothing and knowing not life, into a people who will rule the world with this new-found wisdom, as we enter the 21st century. The many lectures given by Minister Louis Farrakhan are like food, as water is to the earth, and in their publication we pray that they will illuminate that hidden truth, which is necessary to set the masses of the world's poor and ignorant free. Like Jesus said, "you shall know the truth and the truth shall set you free."

The Most Honourable Elijah Muhammad **departed in 1975** and not in 1974 as stated on page ii.

Dedication

We forever thank Allah, who came in the person of Master Fard Muhammad, for His travelling to America to raise One from amongst us, The Most Honorable Elijah Muhammad to give us life when we were poor in spirit and to transform us into the gods, that Allah created us to be.

As Publishers, we would be remiss in our duty of not informing you of the great work of The Most Honorable Elijah Muhammad and the Honorable Minister Louis Farrakhan's servants, here in London, at the West London Headquarters of the Nation of Islam, without whom, this book would not have been produced. In recognition of their work, this book and its compilation are a reflection of the tiresome and endless work of these Labourers, ensuring that in our understanding of the Teachings of The Most Honorable Elijah Muhammad, we get up and 'do for self.'

We also thank Sister Tina X, for her labour's in transcribing and Sister Sonia X for her proof-reading skills and assistance. But most of all we thank the Honorable Minister Louis Farrakhan, for giving us the opportunity to know him, in his work of fulfiling the work of "Elijah."

We pray that these words, spoken by Minister Farrakhan will find a root in your heart, and in your mind; the spiritual house of God, and enable you to see the truths and the reality of these few, wickedly wise individuals and international bankers, who manipulate 85% of the world's population; Black and white, for the purpose of world control, profit and interest.

There is no greater truth today than the knowledge of God, and the knowledge of the Devil, and these three lectures given by Minister Louis Farrakhan during the year 1995, will illuminate the path in your search for the truth. May you find inspiration, peace and joy from these lectures.

As-Salaam Alaikum. (Peace)   Olusola Odesanya X.

THE HONOURABLE MINISTER LOUIS FARRAKHAN

Minister Louis Farrakhan was born in New York on May 11, 1933. His mother was born on the island of St Kitts and his father was from the island of Jamaica. At the age of three, his mother moved to Boston, where he and his older brother were raised. As a young boy, his mother would give him the CRISIS MAGAZINE (an NAACP Publication) to read, as well as the Black newspapers that were available.

He started studying the violin at the age of five. By the time he was thirteen, he had mastered the instrument. Minister Farrakhan finished high school in Boston and attended Winston-Salem Teacher's College in North Carolina. In September 1953, he married his childhood sweetheart, Betsy, and he left college after his junior year to engage in show business and feed his new family. Minister Farrakhan at that time was very popular in the Boston area as a calypso singer and dancer, and an accomplished vocalist and musician. In February 1955, while headlining a show on Chicago's Rush Street called "Calypso Follies," he attended a meeting - The Nation of Islam's National Saviour's Day Convention - and accepted the Teachings of The Most Honourable Elijah Muhammad.

After living in New York and training under Malcolm X, Minister Farrakhan was recommended by Malcolm to head the Boston Temple, where he served as the Minister for nine years, from 1956-1965. In May of that year, just three months after the death of Malcolm X, The Most Honourable Elijah Muhammad appointed Minister Farrakhan as the Minister of Temple Number 7 in New York city.

Minister Farrakhan worked hard in New York, building the Temple to become the strongest Temple in the Nation of Islam. He was blessed to lead the Temple to open 17 businesses, 3 schools, 5 major temples, and a host of satellite temples scattered throughout the New York area.

His unique ability to speak and to make clear the Message of The Most Honourable Elijah Muhammad attracted thousands of people in the New York area to the Nation of Islam. The largest gathering of Black people in the history of Harlem showed up on Randall's Island, May 31, 1974 to hear Minister Farrakhan deliver the Black Family Day Speech. Approximately one year later, in June 1975, before an overflowing crowd in Madison Square Garden, Minister Farrakhan was removed from his position as the Minister of New York City. The departure of The Most Honourable Elijah Muhammad in February 1975, and the assumption of leadership by Imam Wallace D. Muhammad (the Messengers son), brought many drastic changes to the Nation of Islam and to Minister Farrakhan, in particular.

In July 1975, he was moved to Chicago, where after a few months, Minister Farrakhan decided that he would no longer use his voice as a Minister. Due to his love for Black people and his desire to always give them clear guidance and lead them in a direction that would be beneficial to them; he decided that he would not speak when he thought he was no longer in a position to do so.

However, in 1977 after travelling throughout the world, the Middle East, Africa, South and Central America, and throughout Europe, Minister Farrakhan decided, after looking at the worsening condition of Black people, that he must use what God had given him, the ability to deliver the clear message, to lift up his voice to help guide Black people in the only way that he could see benefit coming to them, and that was through the Teachings of The Most Honourable Elijah Muhammad.

Since 1977, Minister Farrakhan has moved throughout the length and breadth of this country (America), bringing the Message of The Most Honourable Elijah Muhammad, unity for Black people. In addition Minister Farrakhan has:

Re-established the Nation of Islam

Retrieved and beautified the National Centre (Mosque Maryam)

Re-opened the schools

Started the Final Call Newspaper,

which is now the No.1 Black newspaper in America!

Established the Clean-N-Fresh programme

Helped Jesse Jackson in his first presidential campaign

Oversaw the campaigns of the first Muslim canditate for congress

Developed the multi-million dollar luxury Salaam Restaurant/Bakery Complex

Regained the Agricultural farm land of the Nation of Islam

Minister Farrakhan has also, in the last few years, made a tremendous impact on the Black communities of America by going into the churches and preaching the unity of our people, showing that Muslims, Christians and people of other persuasions have the ability to join hands as Brothers and Sisters and work together.

Foreword

As-Salaam-Alaikum.

Brothers and Sisters, once again as many times before I have the distinct honour of presenting and introducing to you, one of the greatest Black men to ever be born, The Honourable Minister Louis Farrakhan. There are a few things I wish to clarify prior to our receiving Minister Louis Farrakhan.

Of course our response today is due particularly, specifically to the lies that were written in the Chicago Tribune and is nothing new to Minister Farrakhan and the Nation of Islam. Although we do not object to some of the truths stated in the articles, we do object and strongly reject the wicked lies made on Minister Farrakhan, his family, officials of the Nation of Islam and the entire family of the Nation of Islam which includes all of its registered Members and the forty or so million Black people of America.

The attack on Minister Farrakhan' character was designed to affect the thinking of the Black community who support Minister Farrakhan and the programs of the Nation of Islam, and that support is in overwhelming numbers.

In some way they wish to cast doubt in the minds of those who support Minister Farrakhan by suggesting Minister Farrakhan in some way was hoarding the wealth of the people and that he was using it to support his lavish life style.

Why are you so upset with the economic progress of the Nation of Islam? Why are you so upset that we that love our Leader want to show our appreciation and love by giving to him and ensuring that he lives as, not just one of any kind of leader in the world, but that he enjoys the best that you make. We want to make sure that our Leader is comfortable.

You don't have anything to say about the president of Ford. You don't have anything to say about the Rockefeller's. You don't have anything to say about the Dupont's. You don't have nothing to say about the Kennedy's. You don't have nothing to say about Bush and Reagan and Clinton and all of these that continue to rob our people. But you have something to say about our Leader wearing nice shoes, our Leader wearing fine clothing, our Leader riding in the best that you make.

You know why you're upset? because Minister Farrakhan told you that "you don't have a ladder high enough that can reach up to the heaven to cut off his blessings." This is why you're upset. You want to make emphasis that Minister Farrakhan said that "he owns nothing personally" and that he said "that all of it is owned by you" he tells his followers.

Do you have a problem with Minister Farrakhan having a home in Beverly Hills? The home is not even owned by him, it has been given and is in the name of his wife and his family. The home on 4855 and Hyde Park that you say my father The Most Honourable Elijah Muhammad spent $200,000 [on], you made a great mistake, my father spent $1,3,000,000 to build that home.

And I want to say that Minister Farrakhan told me to tell you that it is better for you to leave him and us alone, because in the name of Almighty God Allah and His Christ, if you continue to touch His anointed one the calamities that you see in America will increase. And you will see more rain, more hail, more snow, more earthquakes the whole country will go down. Leave him alone. Leave the Nation of Islam alone.

Let us prepare to receive our Minister, our Leader, that we love, that we respect, that we support, the Honourable Minister Louis Farrakhan.

Minister Ishamael Muhammad National Assistant

CONTENTS

JESUS SAVES

In the Name of Allah, who came in the person of Master Fard Muhammad, to whom Praise is due forever, the great Mahdi, and in the name of His Servant our beloved Leader, Teacher and Guide, His Messiah to us, The Most Honourable Elijah Muhammad, I greet all of you, my dear and wonderful brothers and sisters who are here at the International Amphitheatre in Chicago, and those who are watching by satellite in various cities of America and the various colleges and universities, and those who are watching by satellite throughout the world. I am so happy to greet all of you in the greeting words of peace, As-Salaam Alaikum.

So much has already been said, I think it is just time for us to get busy. Certainly, I would like to give thanks to all of the Labourers in Islam, our great Assistant Minister, Minister Ishmael Muhammad the son of The Honourable Elijah Muhammad, Sister Tynetta Muhammad the wife of The Honourable Elijah Muhammad for her words, the National Spokesman Dr and Brother Minister Abdul Alim Muhammad, our Minister of Health for his words, and to all of you dear brothers and sisters for this great out-pouring of love, that I have felt over this past week. To the leaders who are present here today, to the teachers and preachers, to the various organisational heads, I am very, very honoured by your presence.

SAVIOURS DAY GIFT

Today is the 40th anniversary of my being given to The Honourable Elijah Muhammad by Allah as a Saviours Day gift to him, to help him in his great mission of giving life to forty or more million of our people in the United States, and hundreds of millions of our people, and others, throughout the world.

Forty years ago on this very day, and at approximately this very time, I was a young musician playing in down-town Chicago at Jean Fadoolies Blue Angel night-club, on Rush Street. I was the featured performer in a show called Calypso Follies. I was known then as the "Charmer," because the songs that I sang and the spirit in which I sang them, were considered charming to those who heard my songs and felt my personality, and therefore the name "Charmer" stuck.

However, as I entered Muhammad's Mosque No. 2, which was then at 5335 South Greenwood Avenue, on February the 26th, I wondered what I would see and what I would hear. I was fascinated by the search procedure and somewhat frightened that they separated my wife and my first child from me, and of course, my wife is seated here with me today, and my first daughter Betsy Jean who went with me to the Mosque that time. And while my wife was seated on the main floor I was in the balcony where I had a direct view of The Honourable Elijah Muhammad.   I later learned that he had me seated in that particular place so that he and also others, could have a direct view of me and how I was responding to the teachings of The Honourable Elijah Muhammad.

Well, being a student of English and having studied Latin for many many years in grammar school and high school, I was somewhat taken aback by The Honourable Elijah Muhammad's splitting of verbs, and what I termed misuse of the language. But the moment that I thought this concerning his speech, he looked up at me directly and said these words "Brother I didn't have a chance to get that mighty fine education that you received, when I got to the school the door was closing."   He said "don't you pay no attention to how I am saying it, you pay attention to what I'm saying, then you take it and put it in that fine language that you know, only try to understand what I'm saying."

I was shocked, because it appeared that The Honourable Elijah Muhammad was reading my thoughts, but little did I know forty years ago, at this very time, on this very day when he spoke those very words, that he was giving me my assignment and foretelling my future. My wife and I accepted the teachings of The Honourable Elijah Muhammad on that day and from that day to this, I have dedicated my life to the rise of our people under the guidance of Master Fard Muhammad, the great Mahdi, to Whom Praise is due forever, and His servant the Honourable Elijah Muhammad, our great Leader, Teacher and Guide.

Now, I came to my spiritual Father forty years ago today in the year 1955. In that same year 1955 our sojourn in America as servitude slaves and free slaves was officially ended, according to the Prophets predictions. Wherein, in the book of Genesis, God said to Abraham "know of a surety, that your seed shall be a stranger in a land that is not theirs and they shall serve them and they shall afflict them 400 years, but after that time," God speaking, He said, "I will come and I will judge that nation which they shall serve, and afterwards shall they come out with great substance and go to their Fathers in peace, and be buried in a good old age."

Now, according to history as written by the scholars, they said we came to America or were brought to America in the year 1619, one year before the pilgrims landed in Plymouth Rock in 1620. However The Honourable Elijah Muhammad pointed out to us that there were sixty-four hidden years of our history, a history that was so terrible, so wicked, so diabolical in its practice, that we were transformed from a people of tremendous quality, skill, wisdom and righteous bearing, into a people that could be typed as sub-human.

AFTER 440 YEARS

The Scripture's of the Bible teach, that this people in the book of Daniel would be stripped of their own names and language, and taught the language of the Chaldeans. The Scripture also teach that this people would be compared to the gold and silver vessels of God, corrupted with wine and strong drink, and here we are. In answer to these great prophecies, The Honourable Elijah Muhammad said to us that the true origin and time of our enslavement in the Western Hemisphere began with an English slave trader by the name of John Hawkins. Some people refer to him as John Hopkins. His father was a great seaman, who prepared the way for his son to deceive us, and bring us out of our native land and people, in the year 1555 on a ship called Jesus.

From 1555 to 1955 is four hundred years. Now here we are in 1995, four hundred and forty years from the time that our Fathers first landed on the shores of James Town Virginia. Now this 440 is a very significant number. The Honourable

Elijah Muhammad said that our Fathers wandered down to the shores saying "you can have this world, just give me Jesus. Give me that ship Jesus that would take me back to my native land and people." The Honourable Elijah Muhammad said that "little did we know that it would be four hundred years before the real ship Jesus, God in person, would come and deliver us from this pressure and from this oppression, and from the ignorance that this oppression had put us under."

The real ship "Jesus," he said, "is God Himself," who would come after that sheep that was lost, and so today I have chosen for my subject, yes the Million Man March, yes Who Will Save the Blackman, but the real subject is, "Jesus Saves."

Now, The Honourable Elijah Muhammad worked among us for forty years. It is historic as well as ironic, that we are here celebrating "Saviours Day," twenty years after we were in this very place. We have not been here to deliver a Saviours Day message in twenty years. Twenty years ago this very day, at this very hour, the poor followers of The Honourable Elijah Muhammad accepted the news that was given, that Elijah Muhammad our Leader, Teacher and Guide was dead.

Twenty years ago on this very stage, the followers of The Honourable Elijah Muhammad hoisted on their shoulders, the son of The Honourable Elijah Muhammad, now known as Imam Wariff D. Muhammad, as the successor to The Honourable Elijah Muhammad. However within three years, everything that we the poor followers of The Honourable Elijah Muhammad had sacrificed to build, was gone. Twenty years later in 1995 we stand in this very place, to say to the world, that God has blessed us to restore his name, to restore his word, to restore his people and to restore our soul. As it is written, "Elijah must first come." Why must Elijah first come? Because Elijah is the trumpet that lets you know that the Messiah is on his way. Elijah must first come and restore all things.

I am in the spirit of Elijah, to restore unto you the things that have been taken from you in this last twenty years. When the old followers of The Honourable Elijah Muhammad, many of whom are sitting here today, saw everything that they sacrificed to build appear to go down the drain, their hearts were broken, and while some of us might want to point the finger of blame to Imam Wariff Hudeen Muhammad, or to others, or to me, or to others, the truth of the matter is written in the Scripture. Jesus in the scripture takes the responsibility, for he said in these words "if I destroy the temple, I will rebuild it in three days." What do you mean pastors? Jesus himself is the destroyer. Jesus himself is the builder, for if except the Lord build the house, we build in vain. So if one was chosen to destroy it, he is an agent of the Jesus, and if another was chosen to rebuild it, he is the agent of the Jesus. I'm just so happy I was chosen to rebuild it and not to destroy it.

So today we want to know, who is this Jesus, who can save? Four hundred and forty years, what is the meaning of such a number? The Honourable Elijah Muhammad worked forty years absent from his teacher, or away from his teacher, Master Fard Muhammad, and it took another four years in preparation for the work that he would do in the absence of his teacher.

THE CONCERT A

So we have forty four years of The Honourable Elijah Muhammad's presence among us, then he departs. Now we are at four hundred and forty years of our sojourn. In music, the concert 'A' that every instrument tunes up by in the orchestra, is four hundred and forty vibrations per second. So if we say, that four hundred and forty vibrations equals 'A', and 'A' is the first letter of the alphabet, so 'A' equals 1, and 1 is the first number of the language of mathematics, then what are we to learn today from this four hundred and forty years, from this 'A', the concert 'A' that everybody has got to tune up by?

What are we to learn from that concert 'A' that is number one, the first note or the first number of the language of mathematics? Here is what we are to learn. We have now come after four hundred and forty years, to the beginning of the establishment of the kingdom of God. It is not that we are to preach the kingdom, we now have the power to establish that kingdom on earth, if we will rise up and take that responsibility.

Everyone must tune up their minds, now I know there are all kinds of thinking in here today, but I'm going to sound the concert 'A' and I want you to begin to tune your minds up to what I'm about to say, because what I'm about to say will give you more power than you have ever had in your life, to make a change in your life and to start from this day forward, not to talk about the kingdom, but to begin to build the kingdom of God on earth. All praise is due to Allah.

'A' represents Allah. "One" represents Allah. You know what this means Muslims? We have evolved into that number "one" which means that we the Muslims, can now demonstrate the power of Allah, more fully than we have ever demonstrated His power in the history of our sojourn in America. What do I mean by that? The Honourable Elijah Muhammad taught us how Allah created himself, and He had to build himself up into the darkness, and ten thousand parts made the One. Jesus comes at the end of the world at the head of ten thousand. I am saying to you Muslims, look at yourself today. We can not even fit in here. The ten thousand is here, and the One is also here with the ten thousand. It is time to get up and go to work and build the kingdom of God.

Now, if we don't tune up, listen, listen, listen, if we don't tune up our actions, tune up our thoughts, tune up our programme on the basis of God, then everything that we plan and everything that we are attempting, will fail. Except the Lord build the house, we build in vain.

WHO IS THE LORD

Who is the Lord that is to build the house? And who are the builders that will build according to the Will of the Lord who wants to build His kingdom in the midst of the decayed kingdoms of this world? This is why we have called this "Saviours Day." A day with the Lord is as a thousand years. We are not just celebrating the birth of a great man on this day, but the man's birth whom we celebrate, brings in with His birth the millennium. A thousand years in which the old world and all its ways will be done away with, swept out, and the new will be established, the wicked are going to be up-rooted and the righteous will be firmly planted. And the Way and the Will of God will prevail over all ideas, thoughts and opinions in the world; "Saviours Day," Jesus Saves.

On every church just about throughout America we see this sign, "Jesus Saves." But the people in the church under that sign are dying from ignorance and corruption, filth and degeneracy, but everywhere we look the talk is, "Jesus Saves." I want to ask my Christian brothers and sisters, do you think; listen good, that by mentioning Jesus' name alone, that this is going to save you? I know the Scripture says "there is no name under the heavens whereby a man can be saved but by the name of Jesus." Well, the name of Jesus is on the lips of millions of people who know not how to save themselves, nor are they aware of the plan that is already being worked out for their salvation. Don't get shook up, just listen. Now listen, calm down.

The true name of a thing is the nature and the function of that thing. So if the name of Jesus is the name that allows salvation to come, then this saving power is not the recitation of the name alone, but the saving power is being in harmony, with the nature, the function, the principal and the programme of the man under that name. This actually is the power, is the work or the function that saves. Unless we come under his name, meaning accept

His nature, His function, His will, His way, His principles and His programme, there is no salvation for any of us.

Well, what do you mean Farrakhan, accept the nature of Jesus Christ? The thing that sets Jesus apart and makes him stand above all the Prophets, is the perfect obedience in Jesus, to the Will of God. Therefore Jesus could say "I and my Father are one." His obedience is from the nature of Him. And unless you, don't say I accept Jesus, a picture by Michael Angelo, of his concept of a pale face, blue eyed Caucasian Jesus. It's not accepting a pale picture, or a Black picture, a dread-locks picture, or a curly haired picture, or a blonde or brunette picture, it's acceptance of the nature of Jesus, to bow down completely to the Will of God. And that's why Jesus said "many of you will say Lord, Lord," and he will say "what, depart from me you workers of iniquity I know you not." OK lets move on.

Jesus represents a body of knowledge, that he asks his disciples to discipline their lives by. In our willingness to discipline every aspect of our lives to the word and the example of the Jesus, to that degree we have salvation. Man, that makes it kind of difficult doesn't it? There's a lot of us in church, you know what I mean, playing church, a lot of us in the Mosque playing Mosque, a lot of us in the synagogue playing synagogue, all in the name of righteous men, Jesus, Moses, Muhammad. Let us stop this foolishness. Unless we are willing to discipline our lives to every aspect of that body of knowledge, brought by the Prophet, to that degree and that degree alone, we have salvation.

Now there is a scripture in the Bible that indicates that each of us has a responsibility to work out our own salvation. Well, if we can work it out, why is there a need for a Saviour? You got a song, "He will work it out." No, He ain't going to work it out, He has worked it out. The question is, are you willing to work it out with Him, according to the plan that He's laid out to help us work it out?

The Saviour comes to give us the means, the method, or the way by which we can be saved. So a man stands up and says "I am the way, the truth and the light." He's telling you, "watch the way I walk, watch the way I live my life, watch the word I speak and then take me as the way, follow me, don't talk about me, follow me." Jesus hadn't told none of you to worship him, he said follow him and that's your problem. You say you are worshipping him, but they ain't hardly too many of you following Jesus.

Now, to the degree that we refuse to work out our salvation, by disciplining our lives to the teaching that we accept, we forbid the Saviour to step in to save and redeem us. What is the meaning of salvation? What do you mean save? Do you who are listening here and who are listening by satellite, wouldn't you want to be saved if you were in a burning building and you saw fire all around you? Wouldn't you welcome somebody who offered you a way out of the building? I think you would.

If you were drowning, somebody threw you a life-line, what are you going to say? "he the wrong colour, I'm not accepting it." You see, when it comes to saving your life you ain't worried about colour. The anti-Semite is not going to tell a Jewish person, "you can't save me." The anti-Black person is not going to say "ah you too Black you can't save me." Once you see your life is threatened you don't care what the colour is, what the race is, what the sex is, for God's sake get me out of here.

The sad thing about this world, is that the world is in that condition. It's under a crushing weight of its own evil, but the world is so proud and arrogant that it refuses to cry out, save me. The leaders are arrogant, they don't know what they're doing. Excuse me leaders, not you, I'm not talking to you, I'm not talking to you Black leaders, no, I'm talking to the high people in power. They don't know what they're doing. But they're too arrogant to say, "Oh man, I don't know what I'm doing, help me."

But the poor, the weak, the dispossessed, those of us who live in the ghettos of America and the ghettos of the world, we know that we are in a terrible condition. Our communities are in total disrepair. We know that we are in need of salvation. The question is, who will save us and by what means shall we be saved? This is why I have chosen this subject, not just who will save the Blackman and why, or the Million Man March, but Jesus Saves. But I want to bring you face to face with the Jesus who saves.

If it is Jesus who saves, this is not a spirit, this is not a spook, this is a real, live human being, but a human being with the wisdom of the time and the knowledge of what must be done, in order to bring about salvation. Are we referring to the Jesus who pre-figured the Jesus of today? Are we talking about the historical Jesus who lived two thousand years ago, or are we referring to the one that he referred to?

JESUS OF 2000 YEARS AGO

Did you know - you all alright? Did you know that the Jesus of two thousand years ago let himself out of this world? How can a man be saved except by a superior knowledge of truth, in a world of falsehood and deceit. If the Jesus two thousand years ago said these words "there are many things that I could tell you, but you cannot bear it now, how be it, when He the spirit of truth is come, He not me," Jesus said, "not me, He will guide you into all truth." Well, if the people of that time, with that man, could not bear the truth, meaning they did not have the foundation to carry the weight of the knowledge that it would take to save themselves. You've got to have a foundation for that kind of knowledge and if you don't have a foundation for that knowledge, God would be unjust to reveal that kind of knowledge to you - listen.

The truth that Jesus was referring to, that would free human beings, was too much for the people of that time. They didn't have the kind of foundation to bear that kind of knowledge, plus the world had to grow and experience so much more of the wickedness of Satan and the wickedness of self. All Satan's wickedness had to be manifest and all our wickedness had to be so great that we would be drowning in our own filth. Wickedness had to reach its zenith which it had not done during the time of Jesus of two thousand years ago. So he let himself out of this. "When He is come the spirit of truth, He not I, will guide you into all truth." This means that the one Jesus saw coming in his name, would fulfil the function that he pre-figured. The nature, the will and the way fully developed, would be in a future man, who would come at the end of the world of the wicked. What would he look like ?

How are you going to tell me, that you are looking for somebody you never seen before and don't have an accurate description of the man? The scripture describes him. He is not Caucasian, no offence, no offence. No racism. The way the Book describes Him He's definitely not Caucasian. The way the Book describes Him, He's not Asian as we know Asians. He's a man of dark colour. He's a man of woolly hair, according to the book He's a Black man. But, wait a minute, wait a minute, wait a minute, I know some of us just lost salvation, just like that.

We don't want it, if He's Black, He can't save me. Blackman can't do nothing for me, but show me which way the white man went. Some of us unfortunately think just like that. Some of us who are Black can't stand to think the thought even, that a Blackman would have the ability, the power, the will and the programme to save us. And there are some white people who have just tuned out right away, they just turned off the television, "Oh Lord, you mean a nigger is going to save us?"

Well if you think like that, you just messed up. See, with us, we don't care if Jesus is a Caucasian. If he were Caucasian I would not have a problem following him. I just would not have that problem. I don't think you would either, would you? not if you're a bigger person that I think you are. You are able to look beyond colour. You've been following white people all your life, so you would not have no problem following Jesus, if he was white. Ah, some of you done got so Black in recent years, but you still go down town and buck-dance, don't you. Oh yes you do, oh yes you do. A whole bunch of buck-dancing brothers and sisters in the name of Blackness. I'm a Black buck-dancer.

No, I would not have a problem following her, if the Jesus were female. I would not have a problem. You see my mother was a woman, I guess yours was too. And my mom taught me very well. So if Jesus came as a woman I would be able to look past biology, because I am not following biology, I'm not following race, I'm not following ethnicity. The programme, the will, the principal, the truth, this is what we got to look for today, no matter who carries it white people. If a Blackman carries it and it's your salvation, accept the truth and live.

However, since the world has crushed the Blackman and he is the most crushed of all the people of colour on the earth, then it seems to me that when you are looking for a Jesus who will deliver, save, reform, reconcile and redeem, you would not think to look for this one, coming from a people, who have been rejected and despised. Nevertheless, the Scripture says "he would come to and from, a people despised and rejected. He would be a stone that all the builders rejected, yet he would be the headstone of the corner." This is not just a man any ordinary man, this is an extraordinary human being. A human being, that is a bridge between man and God. Ah let me talk about Jesus.

He is a human being, listen good, that is a bridge between man and God. He is a human being who breaks down the wall or partition that has separated man from God. He's a human being that allows men and women to access God, in a way that previously, in this world, no prophet could do. What kind of access are we referring to? This Jesus is a bridge that allows us to access the Mind of God, the Spirit of God, to become His own children, that we may grow up, to be and exercise power like our Father. This kind of access was not given to or through any prophet, but is given through this One who comes at the end of the world, who is called Messiah. Who is called "Jesus the Christ."

This one who comes is to raise men and women, from the fall and consequence, of the fall of Adam. Therefore, he is to raise human beings from a dead level and bring them back to the living perpendicular or upright living, according to the Will and Way of God. This then is restoring man and woman to our Godly powers. Godly powers. Oh, brothers and sisters, you have the potential for so much power, but you are not functioning at a fraction of the level of power, that each one of you are capable of attaining.

GOD CAME

Well, how does Satan accept this, a human being coming to be a bridge to help us to access God in a way that no prophet has ever been able to do? Well, Satan is the natural enemy of God. Satan knew that God was coming. Satan knew that this extraordinary human being would be in the world at a particular time, therefore Satan went to work to prepare the people to receive him.

You mean Satan went to work to prepare the people to receive Jesus, sure. That's the question. My brother said "but what kind of reception." Not to receive Jesus with the honour and submission that he was due, but to receive him in a way of rejecting him, cursing him, maligning him, speaking evil of him, that the Scripture might be fulfiled. That you and I would be made so ignorant by Satan that we would take darkness for light, and light for darkness, truth for falsehood and falsehood for truth, heaven for hell and hell for heaven. We would be turned totally upside down, so that the Scripture again might be fulfiled. "He came unto his own, but his own received him not, and the light shined in the darkness but the darkness comprehended it not."

How is he going to come? Where is he coming from? If he's a man he's coming from some place to another place. How is he coming? What will mark his coming? How will you know he's present? What sign will we see of his presence, that we who have been destroyed under the fall of Adam and the deceit of Satan, may find the way to our salvation?

In the book of Habakkuk, in the Old Testament, in the third chapter the scripture says "God came from Teman." Let's stop right there. Teman was one of the sons of Adah. So if God came from one of the sons of Adah, he's a man coming from a man. Therefore he gets the name in the scripture 'Son of man'. Let's talk about it. Then it says, "And The Holy one from Mount Paran, His glory covered the heavens and the earth was full of His praise. The Holy one came from Mount Paran and God came from Teman." Then God and the Holy One are two different men, but two different men coming from two different places, for two different works, at two different times. Listen

Teman is also a city in Arabia. The God of this world came from Arabia. The God of the future world came from Mount Paran. He is known as a Holy One. And the earth was filled with his praise. The name "Muhammad" means "one worthy of praise and one praised much." The scholars of the world admit, that the most significant man in the history of the world, is a man named Muhammad, from Arabia.

He is more significant than Galileo, in the hundred most influential men of the last 6000 years. He is more influential than Newton. According to these scholars he is more influential than Jesus or Paul. Muhammad was the most successful of any prophet on the earth and the earth is filled with his praise, as a sign of a Muhammad that would come at the end of the world. Listen to me good now. Muhammad the Prophet, peace be upon him, filled the earth with Islam. His companions did that. But the Islamic world today has lost the path.

The Islamic world today is corrupted and in need of a reformer. Talk to me. Then who will reform the world of Islam if Muhammad is the last prophet and the seal of the prophet, and the world of Islam has gone to hell? Then you tell me why must a reformer come, if Muhammad is the last one? Talk back to me.

You all say, Jesus of two thousand years ago did the work. Well why are you in the condition you are in? If you know Jesus why aren't you doing his work, in the power of that man? You are a liar, you don't know that man. I want you to listen to me this afternoon. Jesus was not about building a church. You and I can not go back to the Father and say "look at the big church I built," and you're not building people. It's easy to put a brick on top of a brick and slap some mortar in it and say you got a church. It don't take but so much skill to do that. But to take a human being and transform their lives, and put one human being together with another one and mortar in between them, with the love of God and the love of the brotherhood, so that you build up a spiritual house so that the spirit of God can live in the true house of God.

Muhammad and Jesus were a sign of One who would come at the end of the world. "And his brightness was as the light, He had horns coming out of His hands, but there was the hiding of His power. Before Him went the pestilence and burning coals went at His feet. He stood and He measured the earth, He beheld and He drove asunder the nations, and the everlasting mountains were scattered, the perpetual hills did bow. His ways are everlasting, and I saw the tents of Cushan in affliction and the curtains of the land of Midian did tremble." All of this has meaning. He had power in His hands. His presence was as the light. You cannot be in the presence of God or the Messiah and be in darkness, for He is the light. Jesus said "I am the light of the world." Listen. He had horns coming out of His hands, "horns" represent power. He had power but He hid his power, fulfiling the scripture, that He would make himself of no reputation. He had power but He didn't declare his power, not at that time.

"Before Him went the pestilence, plagues announcing His coming," just like the Bible said there would be "wars and rumours of wars, there would be earthquakes in diverse places, there would be pestilence and famine, but these would be just the beginning of sorrows." This is the announcement that somebody is present. Look at the world's condition, wars and rumours of wars, nation rising against nation, kingdom against kingdom. Is that right? But look, He stood and He measured the earth.

The earth is 24,896 miles in circumference. It has a diameter of 7,926 miles. The water of the earth is 139,685,000 square miles, and the land coming up out of water is 57,255,000 square miles. He gave us the knowledge of the rivers and the seas, and the lakes and the mountains. Why? How do you know this? Because He stood and He measured the earth and burning coals went at His feet, meaning every where He went revolution broke out. Everywhere He went revolution broke out. Why revolution? Because Satan, has been sitting over the masses of people white and Black, Jew and Gentile. But when that man begins to walk, revolution would go.

"The tents of Cushan in affliction," Cush is you. Are you in affliction? Everywhere the Blackman is on earth he is under affliction. But "the curtains of the lands of Midian did tremble," curtains meaning, that which blocks out light. Now the people who block the light from coming, they're trembling now, because; Jesus, Jesus Saves, and He is present in the world.

Can you all be patient with me, because this subject is so deep? By the grace of God; it is my 40th year, I got to preach today, if I never preach again in my life, I have got to tell it today.

Matthew, in the book of Matthew, the scripture says how "He comes from the East unto the West as lightning shines from the East even unto the West, so shall the coming of the Son of man be." What's happening in the West, that it demands the presence of God in person? In the West the eagles have gathered together, plucking and eating the flesh of a carcass. Why did he say "where the carcass is, there shall the eagles be gathered together?."

What are you trying to do Farrakhan? I'm trying to get the eagles of the carcass and I'm trying to put life in the carcass in the West. You're the carcass Blackman. And the symbol of America is a eagle and the eagles have picked your flesh clean, and you are more in need of salvation than any people on the earth.

Ezekiel used that terminology the "Son of Man," but Ezekiel saw the Son of Man being set down in a valley that was full of bones; dry bones in the valley, but He had to come as a thief in the night. What night? Most thieves come in the night, but we got some bold thieves today, they rob you day or night. Say in the hood, we know those kind of thieves, they'll rob you while you're looking, "get out that car."

There was a time when thieves waited for night to fall. That's the time when thieves had a little code. Well he came like a thief in the night. What does the night mean? At a time when the wicked who ruled were not paying attention to the predictions of the prophets. They had gone to sleep on their watch and at that time He comes as a thief in the night to seek and to save that which was lost.

Brothers and sisters, is the Blackman lost? Talk to me, talk to me. Are we lost? But what do we mean, "lost"? According to Roget's Thesaurus, when a person is lost, they're unable to find their way. When they're lost they're irredeemable, irreformable, irreconcilable, hopelessly wicked, beyond repair, lost. They're no longer in the possession, care or control of someone or something, no longer known or practiced, unable to function, act or make progress. Are we lost? Spiritually or physically destroyed to be unsuccessful in retaining possession of. Everything you get somebody takes it away. Why? your lost. To fail to win. How many times we going to run for Mayor and not win? Let me depart here for one minute, from my text. Before anybody takes up that kind of challenge you ought to not just look at the numbers, but you ought to look at your ability to excite the numbers. Hell don't run out there for show, because every time you run out and loose you kill the spirit of the people to try again. Mayor Sawyer ran and lost. What's the other brother's name? Evan's, Tim Evan's ran and lost. Judge Pencham ran twice and lost.

I'm not saying we don't have a chance to win, but you got to excite Black people. You have got to stir Black people up. You will never stir Black people up if you're afraid. You will never stir Black people up if your leaders are bought off. You got to make your leaders afraid to sell you out. You have to be able to create so much momentum, that anybody that gets in the way of that train, will be steam rolled over. And until you have that One that can do that, then damn it, stand back and cultivate the field till you're ready. This is no time for personality foolishness. Our people are dying, we cannot play games with them. Our people are dying.

Is the white man lost? I asked a question. White people in the audience you can answer. Is the white man lost? He is lost. Is America lost? Yes, America you're lost. Is the world lost? How did America, the Blackman, the white man, the World get lost? The scripture says "all we like sheep have gone astray." I'd like to change that, no, no, no, we have not gone astray, all we like sheep have been led astray. Who is the shepherd of the sheep, that has led them astray? You have a conflict now with this One who comes to free the people and find them and bring them again. He has to fight against the one who misled and deceived the people and wants to keep them in a state of perpetual loss, that the God in the last days may destroy them rather than redeem them. So the act of saving is to save a people against the force of Satan. To save the people against the force of Satan's wiles and deception. To save the people against Satan's conspiracy to destroy the plan of God for the salvation of the people.

Is America lost, is the Blackman lost, is the world lost? and the answer is "yes." America is lost, she has lost her way, she has lost her moorings, she lost her morals, she has lost her principles. Some would argue that America never had any. Wait, but to those who say America never had any, we could argue back. She had some, but her morals and her principles didn't refer to moral treatment of the darker people.

America couldn't come up from nothing to where she is, except that she followed certain laws, certain principles and certain morality. She had a morality that lifted her and she was lifted by following certain immutable principles. And she is falling now because she has deviated from those principles. Since the whole world is lost, then the whole world stands in need of salvation. So the Saviour who comes must have the wisdom and the power to execute a plan, not just to save a people, but an entire world of people, if they would desire to be saved. But there has to be an instrument through which this plan of salvation is to be implemented.

That instrument is considered a man and a people. He is a man taken from the despised and the rejected and fitted out with a special knowledge and programme that would allow him first, to save a very special, particular and peculiar people. In the plan of God's salvation He chooses a foolish people. I know, I know, I know, if I ask white people are you foolish they'd say "not me I run the world." Chinese are not going to admit to being foolish. Japanese are not going to admit to be foolish. What about you? You know you're a fool. Like Forest Gump said "stupid is, as stupid does" and you know we have done some pretty stupid things, foolish things. Come on, come on.

REALITY OF THE TRUE GOD

So God chooses someone or someone's who [are] at the bottom, that He might affect their rise to the top. He chooses an instrument that is considered the least that He in His wisdom and power might make it the most. He chooses someone or someone's who would be the tail, that He with his wisdom and power may make it the head. Why would He do this? Because Satan has ruled this world, and Satan could never rule by making the true God and his way known.

The only way Satan can rule is by obscuring or hiding the knowledge and the reality of the true God, so the true God in coming, has to make himself known. So He allows a nation to become powerful and great like He did ancient Egypt and in that nation you will find a people weak and insignificant. And He chooses from among the weak and the insignificant in order to make himself known in a world that does not know him. Yes, yes, yes, Jesus Saves.

In Galatians; don't go to sleep. I will take some water and throw it on you, don't go to sleep. In Galatians 4:4,4 now you got that 44 again. Look at what Galatians said "but when the fullness of time was come, God sent forth His Son made of a woman, made under the law to redeem them that were under the law, that we might receive the adoption of Sons." Master Fard Muhammad comes. He comes. Oh, that man right there, let me point to Him. That man right there, you don't know nothing about Him. Well let me tell you a little about Him.

He comes without observation. The government didn't observe him. Those who are the watchers in the society didn't observe him. He came as a thief in the night and He came in sinful flesh to condemn sin in the flesh.

I would like to stop here a moment and talk about what do we mean by sinful flesh? It could mean, that He came in the colour or in the absence of colour, of a people who through sin dominated the darker peoples of the world. I want you to listen to me.

There is no intelligent Caucasian person here in the audience or watching by satellite or in the various colleges or universities throughout America, who will refuse or deny the fact, that Caucasian people; or as they are called white people, came to power over the darker people, not through righteous means, but through means which are universally considered immoral and even wicked.

Come on, come on, don't go to sleep on me now. Alright. Now, most white people don't like it when you make generalities. Nobody does. But in truth, the people of that particular colour or absence of it, are responsible for the destruction of most of, if not all of, the darker people of the world and their way. Whether you came as you say, in the name of Jesus, that didn't make what you did right. You destroyed people in the name of Jesus. You murdered and pillaged and raped and robbed people in the name of Jesus. You deceived people in the name of Jesus.

So since this is true, coming in sinful flesh could mean He came looking like the people who had captured the people of God. That's why when you say we're racist and we hate people who have white skin; hold it, hold it, hold it, you see that man there, we love Him, we honour Him, we respect Him. He looks like a white man but He is not a white man. So don't tell me we hate Him because of His colour. Nobody hates white people because of their colour, white people are hated in the world because of their evil against themselves and the people of the world.

Therefore coming in that flesh He would be without observation. Coming in sinful flesh could mean that the flesh in and of itself, seeks power to satisfy its craving against the moral nature of the human being. I don't want to loose none of you on anything, but if I happen to loose you, or your conscience, or your attention goes somewhere, be sure to get the tape. Because every word that I say today on my 40th anniversary, I am telling you, where I'm going in the next few minutes, Lord I just want you to hang with me.

Coming in sinful flesh, meaning that the power, wisdom of God is now clothed in flesh. God takes on flesh as a human being. Muslims say that's wrong. Hang with me a minute Muslims. He takes on flesh as a human being, fighting the same fight that all human beings fight, to Master the flesh. Now let's look at this.

All Muslims are looking for the coming of Mahdi. The Mahdi is not an ordinary man. The Mahdi is an extraordinary man, but He's a human being. As a human being the power that the Messiah and the Mahdi operate from, is the living power of God. So when they function on the living power and reality and Word of God and they are in flesh, then the "flesh" is the clothing for the Spirit of God.

He comes in sinful flesh. All this Sin comes from us obeying the urges of the flesh. Mastery of the flesh is the Spirit of God aroused in man, to make man a Master of his lower nature. He comes in the duality of the nature of man. Man has a nature that is upright and man has a nature that is horizontal, like that of animals or beasts of the field.

CHILD DEVELOPMENT

You women who don't know how to train your children. You in leadership, in government, who know how to train lions, tigers, bears, elephants, fleas, but you don't know how to train the human child. God says in the Bible "spare the rod spoil the child." It has two meanings, maybe more, but the two I see is that every home has got to function under a rod, a rule, a law, a discipline. Where there is no rod in a home, there is nothing to guide the development of the children in that home.

The other rod is that which inflicts pain. I didn't say abuse. I said pain. My mother used both rods. She said, "I don't know anything about psychology, I have three Ologies that I use, slap-ology, stick-ology and broom-ology" and I think I got the message. And it wasn't her mastery of Freud and Yeung, it was her mastery of slap-ology, stick-ology and broom-ology jack, and I straightened up. Here the government is so crazy, you want to take away the right of a parent to discipline their children. I think if parents abuse the children we ought to step in. But do not deprive a mother and a father of the right to discipline what they brought into this world. That is their responsibility.

You have to train children in their early development just like you train animals, because the first stage of human development is called the animalistic stage of development. And you train animals by things that are good and things that give pain. When they do the thing that you approve of, you give them something nice and when they do the thing that you disapprove of, you touch them with a little pain. So that they know, don't go there, don't go there.

But some of you, you love your children so much, "Ooh I can't spank them, I can't do it, I just can't hit them, I just can't hit him, it's so terrible to hit him. I am just talking to them. Well — hell, you try talking to an animal see if that animal understands. Children in the animalistic stage of development do not understand words. Words don't mean, pain and pleasure mean.

When you've got both them rods and you use them with wis-dom, your children grow up according to the discipline of your teaching. And after a while you can remove both rods, but the rod is now established in the child and the child will only go so far in deviation and then pull back because you established the rod well in the heart, in the mind of your child.

We come into the world like animals and we grow out of an animalistic stage, to a moral stage, then onto a spiritual stage if we are successful in coming out of the animal stage. Those of us - listen to me. You all alright? Those of us who can do evil and it doesn't bother us, you're an animal. I'm going to say that again. You have human potential, but you are in fact an animal.

If you can rob and lie, and cheat, and steal, and cut, and plunder without any conscience, you are an animal. And the Bible calls you a beast or one that has the mark of the beast, because you think like a beast. It's in your forehead and it's in your hands, in the way you work and in the way you do.

In order to come out of an animal stage, we have to be introduced to a body of knowledge that awakens in us a moral consciousness. This is why parents have to watch the children, be an example, and then teach at the right moment, those morally correct principles. Once the child develops a moral consciousness, then when you do evil; not that you won't do evil again, but whenever you do evil it will wake you up at night. It will beat you in your head at night. Are you alright?

RESURRECTION

So, He comes in that duality and really that's what is meant by the cross. The cross has an upright part and a horizontal part. See it, you do not worship the cross you should master the cross. The horizontal nature is the nature in man that makes him act like a beast. The upright part of the cross, is the upright nature of the human being that gives him mastery over his lower self.

So now, when you're on the cross, that actually means you are struggling. That's why Jesus said "can all the world go free?"

Must Jesus bear the cross alone? No, there's a cross for you, there's a cross for me and every disciple of Jesus has to pick up whose cross? Whose cross - your cross. You ain't on no cross. You are, sure, because you are constantly struggling to do the right thing, and don't you ever believe, that it's not a struggle to do right, in a world of wrong. So everyone who struggles to do right, is on a cross.

In the Qur'an it asks the question, "have you seen man who will take their lower desires or their lower nature as a God besides God?" We live in a world where men and women are caught up in the lust for things, at the expense of moral correctness. What do you want? You want a car, how will you get it? What do you want? A fur coat, how do you get it? What do you want, a home? how do you get it? Will you whore, will you pimp, will you sell drugs, will you lie, will you cheat, will you steal, will you get the things that you want over and above a moral correctness?

See, the difference with Jesus, is Jesus said "seek ye first the kingdom of God and its righteousness and all things will be added unto you." Alright, now, now. Well, we live in a world where the lower nature of man has become his God and when the lower nature becomes a God besides God, then we don't listen to the conscious of self, that constantly warns us against our errant behaviour. We crush the conscience if it speaks against the desires of our flesh. And so He comes in that sinful flesh to show us how to overcome as well as master the flesh. And when we master the flesh, we now become master of the grave in which the Spirit of God is buried or is dormant within us.

That is what is meant by the resurrection. Resurrection does not mean somebody dead in the cemetery popping up. Go on out there and try hallowing. Get you a trumpet and blow tonight and tomorrow, ain't no dead people in there getting up now. Some of you don't like this, but your theology is messed up. I have to tell you, that you really do not understand the Scripture.

That body that you put down in the earth decomposes and goes back to the earth. That's not what the resurrection is all about. The resurrection is the trumpet of God; Gabriel, Jabril a man of God, sounding a brassy truth, that goes past the ear of opposition and then enters into the heart, and if it finds the heart a repository for itself, then, the word quickens within man; his true nature, which is the Nature of God.

Then man begins to rise up in the Spirit of God and the Spirit of God begins to condemn his weakness, his immorality, her weakness and her immorality and when the resurrection is accomplished and man has ascended to God, then he has the power to say to his lower self "I'm in control, I know you want to exercise yourself, but I am in control. I feel lust coming on, because that's a mighty fine Sister, but I am in control."

Now, oh Lord, listen, brothers and sisters, brother and sisters you have been so wonderful, so very wonderful to me in listening and the greatest thing that you could give me on my 40th anniversary is not money, but your attention. I know you been here I know, I know, I know and I know you got a lot of things to do and many places to go, but I may not see you again.

I said earlier, God would come to, and God would come from a particular people. The coming to, is the fulfilment of all of the prophecies that God would search the earth for His sheep that were lost and He would go after that particular one that was lost. He would come to that carcass, He would visit among the dry bones in the valley under the name, Son of Man. He would come and be present among them. That's the coming to, but then the coming from, means, that He would find one from among those to whom He had come and He would make that one, His servant, His messenger, His example, to those who yet slept in ignorance. And He would pour himself into that One, then go away leaving Himself in the midst of the people in that One. So now He comes to, then He comes from.

Now the Scripture said "Jesus was raised from the dead." Who are the dead that he was raised from? It's you, it's me. Just as Moses was drawn out of the water, Jesus is raised from a people who were dead and means the knowledge, the wisdom and the power of God, is seen in the last days among a people who were considered no people at all.

Why did you come out here today? Well listen to me, listen, listen. What brought you out here? You are scholars some of you. Scientists, what made you pay $10 for a ticket? It was not to just look at me, was it? You expected to hear something. This is not happening anywhere in America. Something is going on in America. I'm so happy to say to you my beloved Black brothers and sisters of America, that you have been chosen by the Lord of Creation to render a great service, first to yourself and your people, and then to the entire world, that is suffering and in need of redemption.

You have been chosen not because you're righteous, not because you're Black, not because you're good, you have been chosen because of the Grace of God, and your unique suffering; that was preparation and for a divine purpose, to get you ready to receive a high calling, a great mission and a great assignment from God. What is that mission? First you have to go to the lost sheep of the House of Israel.

What is the House of Israel? Where is this Israel? Who are the Jews? Who is this Israel that the sheep are lost in? America is that Israel. The very thirteen (13) stars on the seal of America is the star of David. America is Israel. The Israel in the East, is a reflection of an Israel that is in the West. And the sheep that are lost in the House of Israel, are the Black people of America who are lost under the power of America and her people.

Come on, listen. The Bible says Jacob wrestled with an angel, all night long. Jacob; listen, listen, wrestling with an angel of God. Well wait a minute, wait a minute, if you are wrestling with an angel of God, you are in opposition to God, but not only did Jacob wrestle, Jacob prevailed, wrestling with an angel. Well when you contest the angel of God you are coming with a force and a power opposite the force and power that the angel represents. So if that angel represents God in righteousness, by what power are you contesting Him? And if you wrestle with the angel until his thigh is thrown out of place, then you have prevailed, through the night, however. You wrestled all night long. It didn't say you prevailed in the day, because the night was given to you. And because you prevailed He gives Jacob the name Israel. Jacob was a supplanter. 'Supplanter' means one who is trying to take the place of another, not necessarily by righteous means.

'Israel' means, you prevailed with God. Israel could never have prevailed or Jacob could never have prevailed if God was not with him to prevail. God allowed Jacob to prevail. God allowed Israel to come into existence. Yes, so the sheep of God, got lost following the way of the supplanter. Who did they supplant? See, that Israel supplanted God.

They wanted you to call them what? Master. "Call me master boy." Who's your master? Only God should be our master, but the white man made us call him what? Master. And what is a master? A master is one who has mastered a particular thing, a particular field of knowledge, a particular endeavour or mastered a particular people. And if a wicked man becomes your master, how could you ever become righteous under a wicked master?

THE NATION OF ISLAM

Well, there's an old saying we used to sing in the church "God is going to move this wicked race and raise up a nation that will obe.." That process of the meeting of Master Fard Muhammad with The Honourable Elijah Muhammad, that process brought about the formation of that which is called the Nation of Islam. What is the Nation of Islam? The

Nation of Islam is a group of people committed to obedience to the Will of God, fulfiling what our fathers said, "God will remove the wicked race, raise up a nation that will obey." A nation of obedience. You say it in Arabic, Islam.

This is a unique nation, but how would this nation and this process that is delivering people from the clutches of the power of evil, be accepted by the wicked One, the Supplanter, the rulers of this world. If you notice when any one of us comes to the teachings of The Honourable Elijah Muhammad and accept it, the first thing you notice is a change. Nobody comes to the teaching of Elijah Muhammad and remains the same. You go to church and you join the church, but nobody necessarily notices a change. But our very appearance changes because our minds have changed. Our conduct changes because our minds have changed. Our diet changes because our minds have changed. This is not just a change, it is a transformation in our lives, that is readily noticed by family and friends.

Then you see those of us who accept to become a part of the Nation of Islam, disciplining ourselves according to a body of knowledge that The Honourable Elijah Muhammad brought. And immediately this starts the process of salvation or rescuing us from harm or danger. We come to Elijah Muhammad drunkards, thieves, dope sellers, pimps, whores, murderers, cut-throats, haters, envious people, jealous people, knowledgeable people with no morals, and you see a profound change in our lives. Family life is restructured. Marital relations are restructured. Our homes get saved. We were reckless in the way we handled our money, but the economic principle that is taught by the Jesus, causes you to live within your means and save your home economically. And since the God that we represent is not a poor God, when we follow Him and submit to His teachings, He starts lifting us immediately out of poverty and want, that ignorance has placed us in.

This is all a part of the plan of salvation. He inspires us with a new education, new ideas to form a new educational system. He inspires us to work for our own economic deliverance. So the whole plan of Elijah Muhammad is a programme that spells salvation for the Blackman.

Well, who should be angry with such a programme? Why would the FBI want to destroy a programme that is delivering Black people? Why would the Anti-Defamation League want to destroy a programme that is lifting Black people? Why would the government of America work against such a plan, that would make a people into something that their fathers destroyed, make us whole again make us useful again and give us a sense of personal value?

Why would the government of America fight something like that? Who would fight that? Satan would fight that. Satan would fight it because he doesn't want the people to be saved. There is a song we used to sing in the church, "the devil is mad and I'm so glad, because he missed a soul that he thought he had." Everyone who comes to Christ or comes to God and sincerely seeks to change, Satan comes after them like a roaring lion. What Satan? Who is Satan? I didn't say what is Satan, we know Satan is a spirit and a force that deceives, but who, who; I ain't no owl, 'Who' is Satan?

SATAN REVEALED
(Thessalonians 2:3)

The scripture says "that day shall not come, except there be a falling away first, and the man of sin be revealed, the son of perdition." Who is the Man of sin? not a spirit, who is the man, the man, the man of sin?

The government of America is involved in a conspiracy against the rise of not only our people but the good that we will ultimately do for their own people, and for the world. The government of America is against white people who sincerely work in the best interest of the poor. Satan is in a conspiratorial posture towards this Jesus. Satan does not want Jesus to succeed. Satan does not want to see a true Christian, a truly righteous person, a true Muslim who wants to submit to do the will of God. Satan wants to deceive that person out of the practice of obedience.

Dear Muslims, if I never see you again, I want you to hear me, because I'm goner put something on your plate today, that you can feed on, and it will get you through a dark hour. The government is frightened and when Farrakhan talks about leading a Million Men to Washington, don't you think the government is happy.

If a million fleas showed up in Washington, they would take action against the fleas. If a million mosquitoes showed up in Washington biting people, the government would order a plane with DDT, to spray the city. If a million locusts or bees showed up in Washington, there would be a bee fighting plan. They would be in the war room saying "what shall we do to kill the bees and not kill the citizens." If a million Black people showed up in Washington, how will the government respond? Now listen. The forces of the world that join together seeking to destroy the Nation, also saw in the Nation of Islam small and insignificant as we are, the potential end of their own power if the Nation succeeded.

Do you know, if we succeed in cleaning up forty million people the liquor business is hurt. The pork business is hurt. The cigarette business is hurt. The whore business is hurt. The dope business is hurt. If we just clean up our people a lot of businesses fall.

If we become Muslims and fear only God, we become an army, the like of which has never been seen on the face of the earth. The government does not want to see that. So the government works to destroy the Nation of Islam. When twenty years ago when the Nation took on a change, the government was happy. Talk to me. Why was the government happy? Because we weren't talking Nation any more. We were not setting up the flag of God anymore. We had become intergrationists now. We wanted to carry the flag of the persecutors and the oppressors. The government was happy. They don't mind you stop smoking and drinking, just don't come up with an idea that supplants the idea of wickedness that rules America.

I shall never forget brothers and sisters, I was sitting in a movie theatre in 1977 looking at a movie called "The Lincoln Conspiracy." And in that movie Lincoln is really not killed by Booth. It was a conspiracy right within the government itself, to knock him off, because Lincoln was doing something to interfere with international bankers. I'm sitting in the theatre and while I'm looking at the movie, in my head I hear a voice saying read Psalms. And in my mind I say what Psalms? And the eighty third; a clicker went off and it stopped at the 83rd Psalms.

So when I left the theatre I told my wife. "You know, I had a strange experience." I went home and picked up this Bible, read the 83rd Psalms, "keep not thy silence, Oh God hold not thy peace and be not still, for lo thine enemies make a tumult and they that hate thee have lifted up their head. They have taken crafty counsel against thy people and consulted against thy hidden ones. They have said, come and let us cut them off from being a Nation; that the name of Israel may no longer be in their remembrance." There was a conspiracy to stop us from thinking of a Nation, to make us want to come back and integrate with the very force of destruction of our lives. A conspiracy.

Please, just give me about twenty minutes, please, please. I am literally begging you, just give me twenty minutes. Whenever you talk about conspiracy in America they want to make you a loony-tune, some nut. Many scholars that I talk with say "oh well I don't believe in the conspiracy theory," as though if you believe that there is a conspiracy against the rise of Black people that you're crazy.

Well let me ask you a question. If we believe that there is a
devil or Satan who will act against God, and a conspiracy is
when two or more people act in concert, to perform an illegal,
wrongful or subversive act, then if God comes to plant the
Kingdom of God, because He's on time, Satan must get people
together in a conspiracy to work against the establishment of
the kingdom of God. Whenever we speak of conspiracy there
are those who call those who speak of that, paranoid, sick or
simplistic. But there is a conspiracy on all levels. Please listen.

America the greatest nation in the history of the world was
begun by men who were not the greatest scholars, but they
were men inspired by a common vision, based upon their
understanding and knowledge of the history of church and
government in Europe.

The founding fathers came to this new world armed with that
knowledge, desirous of setting something up that would be
free from the influences that destroyed church and government
in Europe, that denied the right of the people to know what
the aristocracy and the leaders knew. And so the founding
fathers of this nation wanted an intelligent people, to be a
body, that would elect and select their rulers.

The root idea of America, is the concept of Israel as introduced
by the prophet Samuel. That concept of governance failed, or did
not come to full bloom, because of the wickedness of those
people. David gathered the material to build the temple, to
symbolise the nation of Israel. Solomon built the temple, but in
Jerusalem today, we see the last remaining wall of that which
was to be built, as a sign of what God wanted for his people.

The founding fathers of America were heavily influenced by
biblical studies. Studies concerning Israel in particular. They
wanted to build this new nation with safe guards, against those
things that cause the fall of nations and empires in Europe.
The founding fathers built with a kind of morality, based on
principals that were good. Their concept of moral correctness

was for white people. It did not include the Black, the native American, the Hispanic, the darker people of the earth.

Their morality was a limited morality. Their limited vision for America never included that which would become the hallmark of America, her inclusion of all people. America came to be a nation housing every nation, kindred and tongue, race and religion under one government. This has never been done in the annals of history. Rome was an empire that had the world at its foot, but America is a nation that includes the world, and she claims that she wants all within her borders to be included with the rights and privileges of citizenship. But you go anywhere on the earth, and you will see like ruling like, Chinese ruling Chinese, Japanese ruling Japanese. Filipinos ruling Filipinos, Italians, Greek, French ruling themselves. But in America, every human being from every part of the earth, has some measure of inclusion. This is quite a heck of an experiment.

But Thomas Jefferson and others, in writing the constitution; please listen, made a provision that putting the control of money and credit, under the control of Congress was absolutely what the founding fathers wanted, because Congress was the representative of the people. The founding fathers fought against the idea of private control and ownership of a central bank, because they saw how the private ownership of central banks in Europe, caused the undoing of nations, as these banks financed wars, that ultimately caused the destruction of millions of lives.

Thomas Jefferson in a letter to John Adams wrote "I sincerely believe with you, that banking establishments are more dangerous than standing armies." Well what had the founding fathers learned from the history of the activities of privately owned banks in Europe? That history begins with the rise of Myer Anshell Rothschild. I want you to just put on your thinking caps we're going down now into the valley, and I want all of you in this audience, to walk with me.

THE INTERNATIONAL
BANKERS

Myer Rothschild said that "he did not care who governed, so long as he controlled the purse strings." The founding fathers of this nation, I really don't think could be considered anti-Semitic, but Jewish people in the new nation called America, had a hard way to go. But what was that all about ?

Some whites hate the Jews, because of just plain envy, at the success and brilliance of this people, whom God has sent so many prophets to. But listen, when a people are given prophets, the presence of a prophet means the presence of Revelation. The presence of Revelation means that wisdom or knowledge heretofore unknown, becomes known, which opens up new horizons of discovery, new horizons of advancement. If you are the recipient of Revelation, you are chosen by God to be an example of what that Revelation can bring, but you were also chosen to give guidance of that Revelation, to those who do not know it.

The Jewish people have had many prophets, and they have had Revelation upon Revelation. Which means that the Jewish people have been exposed to knowledge unknown in the world before these prophets came, which automatically creates an environment for advancement in every field of human endeavour. For whenever God reveals, His Revelation touches every field of endeavour. It opens up every field. So we should not be surprised that members of the Jewish community are at the head of practically every field of human advancement. They have led the way in science and technology, in all branches and disciplines of knowledge, they are leaders. This can create enmity, envy, jealousy, hatred, plotting and scheming against such people of advancement. Ah, but there's another side to this, that must be understood.

When one receives Divine knowledge; Muslims I want you to listen, when one receives Divine knowledge, that opens up new horizons for advancement upward towards God, there also is the opening up of channels of the darker side of human nature. So when a person has knowledge and refuses moral correctness that comes as a responsibility of those who are possessors of knowledge, then those who take knowledge but refuse moral correctness, become devils. I'm goner say that again devils. I'm goner say that again devils. Black devils, white devils, Red devils, Yellow devils, Green devils, Purple devils. Anybody that is a knowing one and refuses moral correctness, then you will use your knowledge to trick, to deceive, to scheme and you will become a living agent of Satan, the devil.

This devil mentality, works against the advancement of the person toward God, and this is seen in every community where Revelation comes. Muslims is it seen among us? How many Muslims who heard the teachings of The Honourable Elijah Muhammad, that opened up advancement for us, but when The Honourable Elijah Muhammad was gone and we forgot moral correctness, you fell all the way back down, like the dog that you were when he found you? Are you listening to me? "Behold the dog returns to his vomit." So you have men named Sharieff and Muhammad who are dope sellers, dope users, dope pushers, pimps and hustlers. They have become Black devils, agents of Satan. There are Christians like this too, who do their wickedness in the name of Jesus Christ.

Well, in Europe Rothschild claimed to be Jewish. Not the nationality of a Jew, but Jew in terms of belief in God, and a follower of divine Revelation. But was Mr Rothschild a moral man? Here is a man that had five sons and he sent his five sons into five countries. One son went to England, one son to France, one to Austria, one to Italy and another remained in Germany with the father. And from these sons, and the money that these sons had, they worked and manoeuvred and manipulated until they gained control of the central banks of England, France, Austria, Italy and Germany.

The control of these central banks went into the hands of individuals, whose interests were not necessarily in harmony with the best interest of that nation. These privately owned central banks became the printer of the money, and the extenders of credit of that particular nation. So government and politics; I wish the politicians didn't have to go, I wish the politicians didn't have to go, but I understand you're very busy. Government and politics in Europe was always controlled by the money interests. Wars were fought and in order to fight a war, governments had to borrow money.

They borrowed money from these central banks. The central banks waxed rich because they loaned money and charged interest. Then took over when one side prevails against the other, and when governments could not satisfy the indebtedness, then some of the natural wealth of that country flowed to the bankers. They would loan money to both sides in the conflict because they really didn't care who won or who lost.

I mean it's hurtful, that a Jew, Rothschild, loaned money to Adolph Hitler. A Jew, Rothschild. God damn it, you'd better not open your mouth to call me no anti-Semite. Rothschild and Paul Warburg loaned money to Hitler. Hitler killed little Jews, while Rothschild and Warburg stayed in the finest hotels in Europe. But damn it, if you can't call Rothschild anti-Semitic and Warburg an anti-Semite, then don't you open your mouth against me.

In a book titled 'None Dare Call It Conspiracy' by Gary Allen and Larry Abraham on page 45, the question is asked;

"Where do governments get the enormous amounts of money that they need? Most of course comes from taxation, but governments often spend more than they're willing to tax from their citizens, so governments are forced to borrow. The public is led to believe that the government borrows from "the people" through Savings Bonds. Actually, only the smallest percentage of the national debts is held by individuals in this form. Most government bonds, except those owned by the government itself through its trust funds, are held by vast banking firms known as International Banks. For centuries there has been big money to be made by international bankers in financing governments and Kings.

Such operators, however, are faced with certain thorny problems. We know that smaller banks operate to protect themselves by taking collateral, but what kind of collateral can you get from a government or a king? The process through which one collects a debt from a government or a monarch is not a subject taught in the business schools of the universities, and most of us never having been in the business of financing kings or governments, have not given the problem much thought. But there is a king-financing business and to those who can ensure collection it is a lucrative business.

An economics professor named Stewart Crane notes that there are two means used to loan money to governments and Kings and two means of collecting on that money. Whenever a business firm borrows big money the creditor obtains an influence in management to protect its investment. Like a business, no government can borrow big money unless that government is willing to surrender to the creditor, some of its Sovereignty.

Certainly international bankers who have loaned hundreds of billions of dollars to governments around the world command considerable influence in the policies of such governments. But the ultimate advantage; listen to this, that the creditor has over a king or a president is that if the ruler gets out of line, the banker can finance his enemy or his rival. Therefore, if you want to stay in the lucrative financing business of kings and governments, it is wise to have an enemy or a rival waiting in the wings to unseat every king or every president to whom you lend money. If the king does not have an enemy, you have got to be able to create one." Now I'm going to show you why America is in so much debt.

The founding fathers of this nation said they did not want private control of a central bank because to them, such a bank would be the detriment of this democracy. Thomas Jefferson saw a privately owned central bank as worse than an opposing army. Thomas Jefferson wanted to keep America free from those things that lead to the destruction of many nations and governments in Europe. And so a privately owned central bank was unthinkable to the founding fathers of this nation, and therefore it was written in the constitution, that only Congress should have the right to print the money and the instruments of credit.

CONTRACT ON AMERICA

The debt of America is so great that greater hardship is now being planned by the government for the masses of the American people, in order to make America solvent. Please, you know, wake yourself up now, come on, come on. If you got to stand up and breathe, stand up, stretch yourself. I'm winding this down, so come on, I don't want you to sleep now. Are you alright? OK, sit down. Are you refreshed? Good I am too. Let's get rolling.

The great sweep in the November [1995] elections, that brought the Republicans into the control of the Senate, and the House of Representatives, and the majority of the governors' mansions of this nation, sent a message to the government, that the American people are greatly disturbed over the course of this nation, and they all are seeking change. The majority of the American people may not know what change they want, but they definitely desire change for the better.

The Republican party has come up with a theme, they call it "A Contract with America." This contract or agreement is to reform the government in such a way, where great amounts of money can be saved, spending is to be brought in line, taxes are to be reduced. But this contract with America, to many seems; in gangster terminology, to be a "contract on America," where the contract says the poor and the weak must be eliminated. There is no way, that the speaker of the House, Newt Gingrich, or Senator Dole, or the Republican party can solve the problem of the tremendous debt of this nation, without exposing the root of this problem, and the conspiracy that brought America to her wretched debtor condition.

Every home needs a balanced budget. A balanced budget means that we do not spend more than we take in or have debt greater than our ability to handle without over borrowing that will destroy the economy of our homes. Serious financial problems are at the root of most of our domestic quarrels. The tremendous stress on the bread-winners in the American family is such that this stress leads to spousal abuse, women abusing the men, men abusing their wives, the abuse of the children, the break-up of the family.

So balancing the budget at home is one of the keys to a stable family environment. Since this is so in individual homes, it is also true in the large context, the country, the nation. The nation called America, is going towards $5 trillion in public debt. This debt is so great, that in order to balance the budget, such drastic cuts have to be made, that the poor and the weak will suffer the most. So this contract with America is a contract on America's poor. Even the thought of raising the age level, at which time the elderly will receive social security to seventy years of age, is a sign that the social security of those who have paid into it, is in deep trouble. The government if it raises the age limit to seventy, is betting that most of those who paid into this fund will never live to see seventy years of age, and therefore social security will not have to be paid.

This is a disgrace, but what is the root of the problem? How did America get into this condition? You know the President just sent a budget up to congress, of $1.6 trillion. Yet in 1991, the last year that we have knowledge of what America took in, in taxes, America took in a little over $1 trillion in taxes. Which means that if the budget this year or next year is going to be $1,600 trillion (one trillion- six hundred billion), then where will the $600 billion come from, to satisfy the budget?

PRINTING MONEY

At this rate, if America cuts taxes and yet is increasing its budget, by the time Clinton leaves office, if he only has one term, the country will be $6 trillion in debt. At $4 trillion in debt, to pay the interest on that debt in 1991 was $288 billion, nearly one third of what the government took in, in taxes. If the debt reaches $6 trillion, practically every penny that comes in tax revenue, will have to be paid to service the debt, which technically means that the country will be bankrupt.

This condition of great debt has placed America at the mercy of those to whom she is indebted. On page 47 of this same book 'They Dare Call it Conspiracy," by Gary Allen and Mr Abraham, it reads; listen, listen;

"since the Keystone of the international banking empire has been government bonds, it has been in the interest of these international bankers to encourage government debt. The higher the debt the more the interest, and nothing drives governments into debt, like a war, and it has not been an uncommon practice among international bankers to finance both sides of the bloodiest military conflicts. For example during the civil war, the American north was financed by Rothschild, through their American agent August Belmont, and the American south was financed through the Erlanger's, who are Rothschild's relatives.

But while wars and revolutions have been used by international bankers in gaining or increasing control over governments, the key to such control, has always been control of money.

You can control a government if you have that government in your debt. A creditor is in a position to demand the privileges of monopoly from the sovereign"; Oh man this is heavy stuff.

Governments that are seeking money, have granted monopolies; in state banking, natural resources, oil concessions and transportation, to the bankers. However the monopoly which the international financiers most covet, is to gain control over a Nation's money.

Eventually, these international bankers actually owned, as private corporations, the central bank of various European nations. The Bank of England, the Bank of France, the Bank of Germany were not owned by their respective governments as almost everyone imagined. They were privately owned monopolies granted by the head of state, usually in return for loans. Under this system observed Reginald McKenna; President of the Midlands Bank of England, he said "those that create and issue the money and credit, direct the policies of government and hold in their hands the destiny of the people."

Now most of you think, most Americans think, that the Federal Reserve Banking system is owned by the federal government, as the representatives of the American people. But the Federal Reserve bank is a privately-owned banking institution.

On page 59 of this same book, it reads "The Federal Reserve controls our money supply and interest rates and thereby manipulates the entire economy, creating inflation or deflation, recession or boom, sending the stock market up or down at a whim."

The Federal Reserve is so powerful, that the former Congressman Wright Patman who was the former chairman of the House Banking Committee, said "in the United States we have in effect, two governments. We have the duly constituted government, then we have an independent, uncontrolled, un-coordinated government in the Federal Reserve system, operating the money powers, which are reserved to Congress, by the

Constitution. Neither Presidents, nor Congressmen, nor Secretaries of the Treasury direct the Federal Reserve. In the matters of money the Federal Reserve directs them." This was written about 30 years ago, but is it so today?

Recently the chairman of the Federal Reserve board, Mr Alan Greenspan, came before Congress to hint to the Congress, that the Federal Reserve would raise interest rates again. So for the seventh time in a year, interest rates have been raised. The chairman of the board of General Motors and Ford is now seeking an audience with Mr Greenspan, to plead with him not to raise the interest rates any further, and if Mr Greenspan agrees this will be the first time according to what we have read, that the Federal Reserve has agreed to sit down directly with the heads of business. The Federal Reserve sits down with the heads of governments.

Why would business' plead to the Federal Reserve not to raise interest rates? Why couldn't Congress order the Federal Reserve not to raise the interest rates? If you watch Congress when they deal with Mr Greenspan, they don't play with him, because Mr Greenspan is the representative of a Shadow Government that literally dictates the monetary policies of this nation.

Now, do you remember a few weeks ago when the Mexican Peso was in trouble? Against the wishes of the American people and the Congress, President Clinton ordered $20 billion of the American tax payers money to be used to bail out the peso. But who was President Clinton helping? Was he acting on his own, or was he being directed by powerful forces that the American people don't know anything about?

According to what we have read, the bail out don't save the common Mexican peasant. The bail out doesn't save the poor business man of Mexico. It saves the international bankers, who have invested heavily in Mexico. Who ordered the bail out, since the president is supposed to act on the will of the

American people, and the American people said no, and the Congress said no? Who told Clinton you better do it?

You know, The Honourable Elijah Muhammad told us "that the Prime Minister of England may appear to be the leader, but he goes back behind the door to unseen forces that direct his motion, and believe it or not so it is with the American president. The American people feel that voting for the president is voting for the man who has supreme power to direct the course of this nation for the next four years. But there is another power in America, called the Federal Reserve, that is a power unto themselves.

How did the control of the federal banking system come into private control against the wishes of the founding fathers of the nation, and what was written in the Constitution, and what was the purpose of that? Have you noticed how politicians bow to people with money? Well what makes you think that your vote counts? It is money that buys political influence, and oft-times political elections. It is money, special interest, that dictates in a large measure the vote of politicians in city council, in state legislator and in the federal government of the United States. It is the big International Bankers who are in control of many of the world's governments. But how did this happen to America?

The financial woes of this country, produce a ripple effect throughout the earth. The financial woes of America are causing the undoing of the social fabric of this Nation. The people are grossly dissatisfied with the politics and the politicians of America. The people are wondering how the President and the Congress, could loan money to other governments, and give money away with the infrastructure of this Nation crumbling, and the debt is spiralling. How could America give away money when the country is in need? There are millions of homeless people living under bridges, and America is giving away the wealth of the nation. How could America be so, so generous to other nations and so miserly to her own people? It's absolutely, it's a conspiracy.

AMERICA'S FINANCIAL DOOM

And so my beloved brothers and sisters, as I enter my conclusion, The Honourable Elijah Muhammad wrote in his book "Message To The Blackman" that when America went off the "gold and silver standard" her financial doom was sealed. What did he mean by that? When did America go off the gold and silver standard? Who influenced that and for what purpose?

Brothers and Sisters, The Honourable Elijah Muhammad in saying that "when America went off the gold and silver standard, her financial doom was sealed," this is a very big statement, because the financial doom of a nation brings down its government.

When Germany lost the value of the German "mark" the government went down right behind it. Whoever and for whatever reason, America was taken away from the gold and silver standard that made her financial doom something that is bound to happen, then those same traitors are responsible for ultimately bringing about the ruin of the government of the United States.

Now let's close, don't move, don't move. Did you know that from 1900 to 1913 the Federal government had a very manageable debt, into the millions of dollars? But in 1913 something happened. Four things were set up in the year 1913. First the Federal Reserve Bank, the IRS, the FBI and the Anti-Defamation League of B'ini B'rith. All were set up in the same year. Is that a coincidence or is there a tie in? I don't have time to go into all the details, but by the help of Allah I will do that in further writings, if it is the Will of Allah. But it's enough to say, that two German Jews, Paul and Felix Warburg and the international bankers of Europe, wined and dined a Senator named Nelson Aldridge, who was the maternal grandfather of Nelson Aldridge Rockefeller, and they wined and dined him for two years showing him the central banks of Europe.

Senator Aldridge came back to America and was given the job of being a part of the study of the national monetary system. Nelson Aldridge with Paul Warburg had a secret meeting in Jekyll Island, Georgia, off the coast of Georgia, and in that secret meeting what came out of it was the basis of the Federal Reserve Act. They tried to get it through Congress under the name "The Aldridge Federal Reserve Act," but since Aldridge was so tied to the international banking system the members of Congress under the leadership of President Taff, they voted it out.

So they went back to the drawing board and they re-did it and they pushed it through on December 22nd 1913, just as Congress was about to break for the Christmas recess. Wanting to get home quick they pushed it through, and the Federal Reserve act became law. But in 1912 there was a great Presidential election, where William Taff was challenged in his own party by Teddy Roosevelt. Roosevelt was financed by some of these international bankers. They hated Taff for his derailing of the Aldridge Federal Reserve Act, so they wanted to get at Taff, but they felt that a Republican shouldn't bring this Act before Congress, it would be better if it came through a democrat. So these same bankers put money behind Woodrow Wilson, and Woodrow Wilson sold the American presidency to the international bankers.

He was elected in 1912 and in 1913 the Federal Reserve Act became law, and the central bank of the United States was taken over by a group of private banking institutions. Then somebody else began printing the money. Like Rothschild said, "he don't care who rules as long he controls the purse strings."

In 1913 America was not yet at war. In the last Winter solstice of the 6000 year rule of the enemy, America was betrayed by one of her Presidents, and one of her Senators, and one of her members of the United States Treasury.

SYNAGOGUE OF SATAN

Do you know why I'm teaching this subject on Jesus Saves? Because after I say what I'm saying today, if I ain't got a Saviour I am sure going to need one, after I say what I say today. Let me just finish. Do not be frightened for me, you better be frightened for yourself, because some stuff is going down in America right now as we speak, and all our lives [are] in danger right now, and I've got to sound the alarm, brothers and sisters. I don't care nothing about my life it's your life that I want to save.

Listen, now that the bank that prints money is in the hands of private interests, the idea is to push up and inspire the government to borrow. How do you do it? Get America into war. The war in Europe started in 1914 and by 1917 under a lie about the Lusitania being sunk by German subs, the American people were called into a war, to end all wars.

Oh, this is heavy man. I mean you can't believe how wicked, how low down and rotten; now wait a minute, wait a minute, wait a minute, you can't believe how wicked these people are, to play games with your lives and the lives of your babies. Create a war just to get more money, to charge more interest and send your babies to die for bullshit. Excuse me, but bullshit is the dropping of a cow, a bull, its BS, its lies, its deceit and the American people went to war in 1917, and Black people sued to become a part of the war, because we didn't want to be left out of America. So America signed us up to fight the war and Black men died, but they don't know what the hell they were dying for and neither did the white ones know what they were dying for.

But the "Man of Sin" got to be revealed and I thank God that He put it in my heart. I don't have no fear of those bastards, I want to expose them all. God is present, God is in the world and I'm going to prove to you by my life, that God has power to save.

Don't worry about me, you better worry about yourself. Excuse my language but they are bastards, they are illegitimate children of God.

When America started borrowing money they had to have a way to pay it back, and that's how they thought up the IRS. Then they started taking income tax, but by that time the Rockefellers and the Carnargies had their money in trust funds, and they had found a way to get around paying taxes, but the taxes were for the poor and the middle class.

It was a gradual income tax that was to keep on escalating, and in the same year the FBI was established. You think the FBI is out here to fight crime? The FBI have done some of the most wicked criminal things in this country, against the citizens of America. Who are you Farrakhan, that you would take on the unseen powers of the world, to expose them to the light of the day? Who are you? I say I'm your brother. I'm a servant of these two mighty men. [Master Fard Muhammad & The Honorable Elijah Muhammad]

The FBI has spied on and sought to persecute everybody white or Black that tampers with control of the poor people. Whether you're communist, socialist, whether you have an idea that could stimulate the masses with truth, the FBI pounces on you. In the same year that the FBI was established, the Anti-Defamation League was established. The Anti-Defamation League has been used to cover up and to fight against anybody that is not necessarily anti-Semitic, but anybody who will expose those Jews, who have been at the root of the control of the banking system of the Federal Reserve.

So when you start opening up the truth, immediately they call you either a latent anti-Semite or an anti-Semite, because they want to stifle you. They will stifle you, they will drive you out of Congress, they will drive you out of business, they will drive you out of wherever you are, but I say to the Anti-Defamation League this is one Blackman you are not going to drive one damn place.

Now from 1913 to 1995 the debt is nearly $5 trillion, and ask yourself how did we get into World War II? You say that Japan attacked Pearl Harbour. Yes they did, but what were the forces that created in Japan, the desire or the need, or forced them to attack America? You don't know that, but when America went to war after the attack on Pearl Harbour, she had to borrow money. There were the international bankers again. They financed all sides, and how many millions of Americans lost their lives?

Suppose Hitler was trying to destroy the international bankers control in Europe, but he went about it by attacking a whole people. All Jews are not responsible for the evil of the few who do the evil. All Muslims are not responsible for the evil of those few Muslims who do evil. All Christians are not responsible for the evil of those who masquerade as Christians. But certain Jews have used Judaism as a shield.

The Bible says "They say they are Jews, but they are not, and I will make them of the synagogue of Satan," and so all "four" of them are lined up against Farrakhan. These are the dogs siced on those who stand up for truth, the IRS probing to see what they can find, the FBI trying to cajole and trap little cheap Black criminals. In the mosque, sending people in amongst us, to do criminal things and when they're caught ask them, we will lessen your time if you say that Farrakhan told you to do it. The ADL, all of them come out, but here I stand, getting stronger every day.

AMERICA'S DISASTERS

And so like Jonah, God has called you to a great work today. God wants you to go to the people of the modern Ninevah and preach. Ninevah was the only wicked city in the Bible that saved herself from destruction and got two hundred more years added, because she heard the preaching of Jonah. But

Jonah didn't want his job, Jonah was running from his mission, and Jonah jumped on board a ship and fell asleep in the hole of the ship, and the ship got troubled. And the captain of the ship said "save us," and they found that somebody was in the hole of the ship asleep and it was Jonah. So when they threw Jonah overboard, the winds got calm.

Then Jonah ended up in the belly of the whale, and finally after he was in the belly of the whale three days, he decided "I had enough. I've had enough God, just let me get out on dry land and I'll do what you want me to do." So, I'm asking you Blackman have you had enough? America is troubled today because you are asleep in the bottom of America. America is experiencing the worst calamities and disasters because Jonah's asleep in the bottom of the ship, because God got a job for you Blackman. But I'm asking you today, have you had enough? And if you've had enough then it's time to get up and get cast out of the ship. Get cast out of the belly of this whale, but first before you can get on your mission you've got to put on sackcloth and ashes, and you've got to repent for being so slow in accepting your duty, and your responsibility. You've got to repent for being the fool, the clown, the buffoon, the pimp, the punk, the hustler, the buffoon, the clown. You've got to repent. You've got to atone.

The social fabric of the house is being torn apart. The country is suffering increasing calamities. God is angry. So the only real saving power for America is that human being in the Bible, that is called Jesus. But really in truth my dear pastor, Jesus can't save, only Christ can save. You see, Jesus couldn't save as Jesus, he had to be exalted to the right hand of the father, then given power, then that Jesus, the Christ, became Saviour and Lord for all.

To know Jesus of the Gospels is not to know him in his exalted state, but to know him as he is exalted to become the Christ, that is to partake of the wisdom and power necessary to turn the weak and the negative thing into strength, and that which is positive. The Christ principle is the only thing that can turn America around and save this nation, but the American people have to recognise that is there is a conspiracy, and the American people have to refuse to take part in it. And whether the whites refuse or not, you've got to refuse.

You've got to refuse to be a sex hound. You've got to refuse Black woman, to be a street urchin. You've got to refuse to let men use your body for pleasure and disgrace you as a woman of God. You've got to refuse Blackman to pick up a gun and kill your brother over the wrong colour, or the wrong sign or the wrong gang. You've got to refuse to be a part of the madness, and you say, "but, but, but I need money man, I ain't got no job man." Shut up! Don't come to me with that punk excuse. God came and offered us money, good homes and friendship in all walks of life. I've got money, I've got a good home, I've got friendships in all walks of life and I'm neither a pimp, nor a hustler, nor a thief, nor a liar.

THE MILLION MAN MARCH

This is why I am calling on us to take the vanguard position, and march on Washington. That's why I'm calling on the Blackman all over America, to stand up like a man, and be a man, and let's go to Washington on behalf of our suffering people, and say to America, we demand justice. Justice for the poor, justice for the locked out, justice for the weak of the nation, but first we've got to atone. We've got to repent, so on October 16 1995 we are going to call it a Day of Atonement.

A million Black men coming to Washington in the name of God. Men of God, atoning for our wickedness in refusing to accept our responsibility to do something for Self. Atoning for putting our women and children on the front line, to fight bleed and die for our advancement, while we as men stayed at home. Atoning for what we've done to one another, to make our communities what they have become, and then accepting our responsibility to do something for Self.

We must march on Washington, ask the FBI and the government, and the Justice department, open up the books, let us see who killed Malcolm. You want to pin it on me because you see me rising. You see Black people listening and you don't have no Black person to challenge me. So you going to raise my brother from the dead, and then make me an accomplice in his murder to kill the influence that Farrakhan is developing with the young people. The FBI is a part of the conspiracy.

How dare you go and trick my sister Quibillah Shabazz and manipulate her pain, after you have manipulated the situation that caused the death of her father. Now you want to put the daughter in jail. How low down and rotten can you get?

Linden Johnson fabricated a lie called the "Tunkin Gulf" incident to get us into the Vietnam war. And they had to borrow money, and it was the Vietnam war that sunk the economy of America. She'll never recover from that hole. And look at the lives that were lost, the people that were wounded, that came back from that war destroyed. I'm telling you government you are not getting none of mine to fight in one of your damn wars. And I'm telling you Blackman of America stay out of America's army, stay out of her navy. If you want a job come on to God, and let God put you to work. Don't let America send you all over the world to fight wars for the international bankers.

You're wearing all your African clothes, how proud you are of Africa. Africa's a bigger slave today than she ever was. Did you hear what I said? Africa owes $400 and some odd billion in debt, to the international banking institutions of the world. And they have taken control of the policies of many governments directing them. And now they have a grip on the natural resources of African countries, because of Africa's debt and her weakness to unify and get out of that debt.

I say we've got to march. We have got to show the world that the Blackman of America is alive and well. That the Blackman of America is finally standing up, to shoulder our own responsibility as free Black men. And so as I leave you I took this subject "Jesus Saves," because God wants to make me an example of His power to save. He wants me to love him enough that I would be willing to give my life. Because if you are not willing to die for God He can't use you. If you are not willing to give up everything you've got for God, He can't use you.

I thank God for the life that He gave me. I thank God for the time, I thank Him for my wife, my children and my extended family. I thank God for the time he has allowed me in His universe, to behold its magnificence. I thank Him and love Him with all my heart, with all my soul, and with all my mind, and I'm ready now, to go down into the valley of death and challenge the force of death for the liberation of all of our people. But I know, that ye though I walk in the valley of the shadow of death, I will fear no evil, for Allah is going down and His Christ is going down in the valley with me, and I promise you in the name of Allah that the last enemy that we must conquer is death. And when we conquer death, on the other side of that is the kingdom of God and its establishment, and I want to go in front of you, but you have to come behind me.

You've got to challenge the forces of death. Nobody, nobody, nobody, nobody should be afraid to die, but today we've got to challenge death. The international bankers, the wicked manipulators, the real Satan's of the world, we've got to upset their world, upset their kingdom. I am set before America as a dare. I know, that if you kill me, I'll be the last Blackman that you ever kill.

Don't fear for me, don't worry about me, I'm alright, I'm in the bosom of the one you call Christ. I'm in his bosom, I feel His presence all over me, all around me. So He said "who will go for us," and I said "here am I, send me." I'm anxious, I thank God for the womb of my mother that brought me into the world to trouble Satan's kingdom. I want to help to tear it down. I want to help to build a new world where people can be free, justified, and equal, and live in peace and in harmony with one another.

So if you will march with me in a Day of Atonement, cry out to God for justice, then God will give you the vanguard position. Rise up and take your responsibility. And so I would ask the Muslims, but in asking you I am asking all of our people in general, that command that Jesus gave knowing that he was facing the cross, but also believing deeply in his heart that he would be delivered from death, he said to his followers and through his followers to the world "love ye one another, even as I have loved you."

He had come to the end of a particular phase of his journey, and he had demonstrated to his disciples how much he loved them, but he knew that the disciples were weak, because they were filled with strife, and envy, and contention, and jealousy, and they all wanted to be at the right or the left, or to be in front.

He knew that it was alright to love him, but the best way you could show that you loved him was to practice that same love for one another. I say to the Muslims, that I have proved to you that I love you. I have not taken your money to deceive you. I own nothing in this world. Every thing that I have belongs to you. I put my name on nothing, it all belongs to you.

So there will never be no fight over me if I'm taken, as to who owns what. You are the owners, and everything I build, and we build to the old followers of The Honourable Elijah Muhammad, it is yours too. This Saviours Day I offer the farm, I offer the restaurant, I offer it all, to all the old followers, who suffered to build with Elijah Muhammad, but you can't have it, unless you respect Master Fard Muhammad and you can't have it unless you respect The Honourable Elijah Muhammad, and come on home and work for the deliverance of our people.

So I appreciate all the love that you have poured on me this week and these many years, and I thank you on behalf of my wife and my family. I thank you for all the love you have shown us, but it does not mean anything to me, unless I can stay behind the door, and see you showing love to one another. The least little believer, show them the same love that you show me. The least little Black brother or sister, lift them up as though they're a king, because in God's eyes they are kings, and if you would do that, we will constitute a Nation that will never be removed from the earth.

So I thank you for enduring these hours with me. I thank you for listening to me, and I pray that God, will Bless you with the happiest of Saviours Days, and that the Saviour will walk with you, and me, and us, and redeem us and reconcile us, and restore us, that we may go on this mission for Him, with all of the lost peoples of the earth.

Thank you for listening, as I greet you in peace.

As-Salaam-Alaikum.

I Will be the
Winner Living or Dead

In the name of Allah, who came in the person of
Master Fard Muhammad, to Whom praise is due
forever, we thank Him for raising in our midst a
Divine Leader, Teacher and Guide, the Messiah, The
Most Honourable Elijah Muhammad. I greet all
of you, my dear Brothers and Sisters, with the
greeting words of peace As-Salaam-Alaikum.

MEDIA MOTIVES

To Minister Ishmael, to all of those who spoke prior to my entrance, I thank you for your defence of yourself and of me and of us. I am grateful to all of you who arepresent who came out to hear what we have to say. While I am thanking everyone I would like to give a special thanks to the Chicago Tribune - no, no, I'm not joking. I thank the Chicago Tribune for giving me and the Nation of Islam four days of "front page," and an awful lot of space in such a well respected journal.

Although I don't think their motives were necessarily to help me or us, the articles I believe have indeed been helpful to us. The Honourable Elijah Muhammad one day told me about a donkey that fell in a ditch, and everyone that came by threw a stone at the donkey, and they threw so many stones that they filled up the ditch, and the donkey walked out. So he told me, he told me to remember that every knock is truly a boost. Because of the one-sided nature of the reporting it is clear to me and to us, that the intention of the Tribune was really to hurt Louis Farrakhan and the Nation of Islam. But of course, help as well as hurt are in the hands of God. I do not believe that your articles accomplished what they set out to do, regardless to the intent. I really sincerely, personally thank you for what you have written.

I wish to turn our attention to the importance of a free press in a democratic society. One of the reasons that a free press is important is that it allows the members of the fourth estate or the press, to search individuals, groups, parties and persons, to see whether they are what their public persona might lead us to believe they are, and to discern the truth of persons; the truth of groups and organisations and the good and ethicacy of ideas. But most importantly their function should be to search those who would deceive and rob the people of their rights in a democratic society.

Unfortunately today corporate America has taken over much of the print media and much of the media. Therefore much of what is written is really coloured, not just by writers and editors, but by those who are owners, stockholders and the manipulators of the minds of the masses of the people. It is not an accident that Jesus referred to the people as sheep. This is the characteristic of the masses of the people, not just Black people, but the masses of the people Black and white, Jew and gentile are like sheep. Easily led, sometimes in the wrong direction. So when you have control of what is fed into the mass mind, then you can dictate the current, the motion of people.

That is a great responsibility, and it is a responsibility that should be carried out by the members of the press with the same kind of sacred aura as being a judge, to judge the affairs of men. In the Holy Qur'an we are admonished not to mix up truth with falsehood, nor hide the truth while we know. It is very important for newspapers to understand, that when you mix truth with falsehood, hide the truth and then outright lie, you are absolutely destructive of the human mind and spirit.

The Honourable Elijah Muhammad taught us that the brain is constructed to think rightly, and the only way we can think rightly is if the brain is fed truth. The universe is created in truth, it feeds the right things to the human mind. But we are just not under the influence of what God has created, we are also being influenced by Satan and his machinations. And so newspapers and television media and those of us in leadership as well, must not lie to the people.

We must not mix up truth with falsehood. We must not seek to deceive the public with a false impression of who and what we are, because when they do that we are destructive of the human mind and spirit. Those who read what you write, if it is mixed with falsehood and then you purposely delete or hide the truth, then you and I who do this, any of us who do this, are partakers in the destruction of the human mind and spirit, and partakers in Satan's conspiracy, to deceive and rob the human family of its inalienable right to truth.

Every human being has a right to truth, and it is only when we know the truth that we can make proper decisions for our lives. So those who are in leadership to whom the people look for guidance and truth, must never allow themselves to be co-conspirators with Satan. So those of us who have read this series of articles and much of what is written about the Nation of Islam in the American press and the World press, we know in some cases it is an outright lie, and in some cases it is truth mixed with lies.

In the Chicago Tribune article there are outright lies, then there are truths mixed with lies. But only those who know the truth can discern the lie from the truth. Those who do not know the truth; and that's a broad mass an unsuspecting and gullible public, may eat this poison food and end up thinking the wrong thoughts, and perhaps taking the wrong action.

Let us just delve a little into motives. Why do we do what we do? See, the motive of a person tells us the condition and quality of their heart. Only God knows the heart, but we can get an indication if the heart is diseased by studying actions and comparing actions to words, and then comparing it's actions and words to a standard of decency and moral correctness.

What was the aim of these articles? Why would you take up all of this space in such a fine newspaper, and give the Minister headline? I didn't rape anybody, rob anybody, shoot anybody, I didn't accidentally fall off of a bridge, or jump off a skyscraper and begin to fly, but I received headline, front page treatment. What was your motive? Why are you worried about what I own?

Since no one has charged me with being a thief, why are you worried about what I own? I know, I know what you said, you said "he's taking money from the poor." Oh stop it, stop it. Now, I don't take as much money from the poor as the Tribune, and I'm a lot more faithful to the truth. Let's be honest. What are the odds that those of you who buy the lottery will win? Come on, come on, let's deal with a little truth, let's see who's taking money from the poor.

Every one of you that; who buys a lottery ticket, the odds are staggering that you will never, ever, ever, hit the lotto. And you know this, but you continue to play because your hopes are maybe, maybe, just maybe. And somebody is gambling that you are going to continue to hope and play that lotto, and poor people are depriving their children of necessary food and clothing because they have a hunch that their numbers going to come up right this time. And then should one, or two, or three of you hit the lotto, look at the way it is arranged. You get it over a twenty year period, you can't even pass it on to your heirs, to your children, think about this. And they're wagering that the quick money will so alter your lifestyle that you won't be able to handle it, and most won't. So before twenty years passes, maybe within five to seven years, the lotto person that hit is dead, and you gamble knowing that they will never see twenty years.

Who's taking from the poor? Who's robbing the poor to enrich themselves? How was America built? Was it built on the backs of the rich? Or was it built on the backs of the poor? How is every nation in the world built? It's built on the backs of the poor, but the poor supports Farrakhan, not because I'm a thief and a robber. The poor support me because they know that I am just about the only one standing up.

And if I live in Mr Muhammad's fine home, not mine, the next leader of the Nation of Islam will live there. Why do you begrudge me that? When I lay down at night in a comfortable bed there's nothing wrong with that. If I drive a nice car, wear nice clothes, nothing wrong with that. If I were poor, ragged, hungry, naked and out of doors you would have something to say about that, wouldn't you? You'd say "well what kind of man of God is this, hasn't God heard his prayer lately?" I got a God that hears my prayers and I have never prayed for money. I have never prayed to live in a nice home, I have never prayed for things, I have always prayed to God to increase me in knowledge and wisdom, and understanding and power, to help my people out of the condition that the blood-suckers of the poor have put my people in.

What is the motive? The motive is hatred and at the root of the hatred is envy. For ten years now, eleven now, you have lambasted me, maligned me, ridiculed, mocked and slandered me, in hope that my own people would turn aside from me, and that perhaps one from among my people, or a group from among my people would assassinate me.

You hoped that we would never earn money in your society to do anything of value for ourselves and our people. You are absolutely livid with anger that we have succeeded in spite of all of your opposition. You have not been able, thus far, to stop funds from coming to the Minister, although that's what you are busy doing.

The ADL has been busy going to every college president, particularly the Black ones, telling them "don't let a Nation of Islam speaker speak on the campus." Because they don't want any of the Ministers or representatives to get a honourarium that perhaps some of it might come into the coffers of the Nation of Islam. College presidents are getting letters like this from the ADL.

The ADL had no standing whatsoever in Congress to bring us before the Congress. They didn't have standing, but they used their influence to bring us before Congress, then when we won they said they got sand-bagged. Well you should expect sand-bagging when you come up against Louis Farrakhan and the Nation of Islam. You should expect it.

A BLACK MAN RISING

So your angry that Brother Farrakhan is able to live well. Die in your rage. You are angry that Farrakhan is being successful. You are angry that over $5 million was raised by poor people to establish the Salaam restaurant and bakery complex, and we did not have to ask you for anything. You are angry, you are angry. I understand, you want to stop whatever flow of charity there is coming to me and the Nation of Islam, and you want to do it by any means necessary.

Your frustration comes out in your writing, the hatred comes out and is manifested, but underneath the hatred and the envy, is the sheer terror. Terror! What are you terrified about? What are you afraid of? You're terrified of a Blackman rising in this country, a Blackman over whom you have no control. A Blackman that you can't frighten away from the platform of truth. A Blackman who appears to be getting stronger every day, with the help of God, and now the things that this Blackman is saying and the persons whom he is exposing; who are so powerful, you are terrified by the truth that he speaks. "Will he lift the cover on me today?" So you feel that at all costs Farrakhan must be silenced.

Well, I would like to invite you at this point to a challenge. Whatever you think you know on me and of me, hurl it at me. Whatever the powerful insiders, international bankers, establishment, secret government, whatever you wish to inspire the legal government to do, get busy, get busy, go on and do it. We have you now in our grip. Some of my Black brothers and sisters want me to be quiet, be silent, I can't let them go and they can't let me go. I can't let them go. God has me on your behind and I'm not going to let it go, and you got me like you're holding on to an electric current, and you can't let me go. So we are locked in a life and death struggle, only one of us is going to survive.

Now I want you to write this down. I shall tell you today straight up, with the help of Almighty God, I am going to be the one to survive, and those who oppose me, Black or white, Red, Yellow or Brown, high or low, you are destined to meet ruin, disgrace and total destruction. Write that down. I'm going to be the winner living or dead. And personally speaking, I don't think you can kill me, that's punk stuff. You did that yesterday. But I don't think that you'll be able to put that small time stuff over on us today, not with God present. But you try, help yourself to your own destruction.

You know there's this wise man in the Bible named Gamaliel, he was a legalist, a great scholar of Jewish law, and he told the Sanhedrin; Jewish scholars of that day, it would be wise to leave Paul, the great preacher for Jesus alone. He was wise enough to say to them "if the work of this man Paul is from man or of men it will come to nought. But if his work is the work of God and we oppose it, we will find ourselves opposing God, and in so doing bring ourselves to nought." Well, you are faced with the same condition and predicament today.

Every thing you've tried to hurt me, and to hurt us, has failed. You the smart ones in your smoke-filled rooms with all of your fine degrees and all of your power, and yet everything you have tried to do, to hurt the Nation of Islam has failed. Ain't you got any sense at all? Don't you think you ought to stop a moment and ask yourself how could these half illiterate people cause you to fail with your power, your wisdom, your money, your organisation, your control over the minds of the people? How could you fail?

Don't you wish to believe that perhaps, God is with us? Perhaps Farrakhan not just some passing fancy that you can blow on and he'll blow away. So you keep on trying and the more you try such evils the more you get tied up in your own deceit. Now the whole of America will soon be made wise to this wicked group of people, whom it is my duty to expose, that the masses of the people, Black, white, Hispanic, Native

American, Arab, Asian, African, Jew and Gentile may go free. For it is written "you shall know the truth and the truth will make you free."

What truth should you know? Oh Brothers and Sisters, you should know the reality of God and His presence today. You should know that the reality of God, is the manifestation and reality of the Devil. You've got to know both rulers today. You got to know God and you got to know the Devil. You've got to know the time and what must be done. You have to know the true religion of God and you have to know this handful of wicked families, that are hell-bent on ruling the world, and hell-bent on the destruction of America.

This handful of wealthy people who have gained their wealth by sucking the blood of the poor, poor whites, poor Blacks, poor Hispanics, poor Native Americans, poor Jews, poor Gentile, poor Asians. This group of families they have no commitment to anything, except their own desires to rule, and to manipulate those whom they rule for their own evil purposes.

The Honourable Elijah Muhammad has taught us, and it is now my duty as a free man to point out to you, that you may rise up, Black and white, poor and not so poor, to ease up, take control of America for yourself, or your country right now is all but lost. Your leaders many of whom are wise to the conspiracy that has robbed America of her greatness, but they have sold you out. I'm speaking of the white leaders, the Black ones we know where they are. The white leaders who know the truth and have no courage to stand for the future of this Nation have already sold America out.

The leaders who know the truth and many who wish to tell what they know have been silenced. But today by the Grace of God, there's a Blackman in America, who is in the bosom of God, who is unafraid to tell you that truth, that will cause you to regain your self and perhaps regain your Nation.

BALANCE OF POWER

Russia is all but gone, destroyed now with internal division and chaos. This is not an accident, this was by design. But who is the designer of the fall of Russia? Because the same designers who designed the fall of Russia have already designed the fall of America. And God sits back watching and manoeuvring to make sure that it all fits His own plan. Russia was financed by the international bankers of Europe and America. Trotsky and Lenin got their training and their money right here in America. Lenin left America with $6 million in gold, financed by those same international bankers, to go back to Russia to begin what is called the Bolshevik Revolution that brought the Communists into power.

Let's talk, I ain't got time to tell it all, but I'm going to tell enough of it and then you can go and find the rest. All of it is written in a book, but you had better become readers now, your very life depends on your willingness to read. The international bankers have always wanted what they call a balance of power in the World. Let's talk, let's talk. As I told you at our Saviours Day message, which if you don't have it be sure to get it, it's part one of this subject.

The Warburg's, the Rothschild's who financed Hitler; German Jews financed Hitler right here in America, Loeb and Kuhn and Jacob Schiff. International bankers financed Hitler and poor Jews died, while big Jews were at the root of what you call the Holocaust. Why don't you tell that one? You can't write this. Go back and tell your editor "I want to put this in the paper tomorrow." You've got a hell of a nerve to open your mouth to call me an anti-Semite when your own people have been the worst anti-Semites in the World. Ah sit down in your seats, we ain't going nowhere for a while. We going to tarry here till we get the Holy ghost. What do they mean 'Balance of Power'? This is how the international bankers get their money back from governments whom they have loaned the money to. They manipulate the sovereignty and gradually take it away from you. They finance an opposing force. They create the opposing force, then finance it so that there is a so-called balance of power in the World.

As you recall my Saviours Day lecture, some conspirators in America, in Congress, met at Jekyl Island in Georgia with Paul Warburg, Van Der Lipp, Nelson Aldrich the maternal grandfather of Nelson Aldrich Rockefeller - a member of the US Treasury, and they designed what later became the Federal Reserve Act. It didn't pass at first because America never wanted a central bank to be controlled by individuals. That was in the Constitution and it's there now, that only Congress should have the right to print currency and the instruments of credit.

But the international bankers, from the House of Rothschild, who sent his sons into five countries; one son went to England, one to France, one to Austria, one to Italy and one stayed home in Germany with the father. And through manipulation and money from that one son, they gained control of the Bank of England, the Bank of France the, Bank of Italy, the Bank of Austria and private concerns began to print money in Europe.

The Rothschilds would finance both sides of all the European wars. They always wanted to get their hands on the central banks of America, and they finally did on December the 22nd 1913, Congress passed into law the Federal Reserve Act. Two months earlier Congress and the same manipulators who crafted the Bill that would later take control of the central bank of America, they also crafted from the second plank of Karl Marx's' Communist manifesto, what they call a graduated income tax.

The income tax was designed so that when America's debt would get greater they would have a means of taxing the people to pay the interest on the debt. Now let's talk. Woodrow Wilson sold America out. Your president. He got in in 1912 financed by international bankers. In 1913, the

Federal Reserve Act was passed, and in the same year the IRS became law. In the same year the FBI was established, and in the same year the ADL came into existence. This is not an accident, these four work together. I'll prove it in a minute.

AMERICA IN THE WARS

When Woodrow Wilson became President in 1913, just before the Federal Reserve Act became law, America's national debt was nearly $1 billion. When Woodrow Wilson left office in 1920 America's debt had risen eight hundred percent, from $1 billion to $8 billion. How did the rich make America's debt grow? The easiest way to get money is to start a war. Woodrow Wilson campaigned on the platform that he kept us out of war, because the war had started in Europe. And if you remember George Washington and the founding fathers did not want America to be involved in Europe's' wars, because it looked like Europe was fighting every few weeks, and the bankers were getting big, big money.

But the moment the international bankers took control of the money by taking control of the central bank of America; the Federal Reserve, a war broke out in Europe. And the British sent Lord Weisman to America, to encourage America's involvement in the war. The Germans didn't start any war with America. Let's deal with truth, because your government is filled with liars and thieves, and murderers and it's time now that somebody take courage and expose it, that all of you will go free. Well you can put your pens up I know that this is a little too hot for you to handle. I'm just warming up.

This man Woodrow Wilson campaigning to keep the American people out of the war, he won re-election in 1916. Five months later, even though he campaigned on keeping America out of the war, five months later he reversed himself and they used the sinking of the Luisitania. Here ammunitions were being sent on a ship that passengers were on. The Germans took out adverts in the American newspapers, "Don't get on these ships because they're carrying ammunition and if you do, you get on at your own risk." So the ship was sunk by a German submarine and this was the pretext.

Then of course, the Federal Reserve who manipulate media; now I'm going to show you how you all don't have no media, that is really out of control. You are not the controller, oh hell no. Some of you little sincere people "I'm going to write the truth." If you want to write it, you had better get your own paper, for you won't be able to write truth in a Negro paper because the editors and publishers are frightened to death that they will lose their advertisers.

You know I'm telling the truth, and most white news; I'm talking about the big ones now, there's somebody calling shots. We'll get to that in a minute. You're going to wish you had left me alone. I'm not going to ease up, I'm not going to ease up. From now on every time I open my mouth I'm going to tell more and more, and more and more, and more of the truth, that exposes the rottenness of all of these confederate forces, that are the destruction of my people in particular, but the masses of human beings in general.

Now let's go back, 1917 America gets into the war. At that time $1 billion in debt, now America got to borrow money to finance the war effort. Whose she borrowing from? Who is America in debt to? She jumps in the war, the war is won and the politicians say 'It was a war to end all wars'. Were they telling the truth? How could they be telling the truth when Jesus said "There would be wars and rumours of war, and Nation would rise against Nation, and Kingdom against Kingdom, but this is just the beginning of sorrows?."

How could a so-called Christian campaign on a slogan that is against the prophecies of Jesus Christ? And how could Christians who say they believe the Word, vote for an out right liar, if you believe in Jesus? Well you all are something, and really in truth you are good people, but ignorance is our worse enemy. And because we are ignorant we are easily manipulated by the wise, smart, crooked, deceivers of the world. I'm going to move fast.

After World War I was over; now listen to this, Max, Felix and Paul Warburg, all three of them brothers, Max, Felix, Paul, and Lord Milner, another financier of Hitler, they met representing their countries at the Paris Peace Conference. See, after the war was over these same bankers, they're going to carve up Europe now. Now listen, listen, listen, let me just slow down a second. I don't want to take too much. But you see all these border wars going on in Africa, in the Middle East, in Europe, what do you think that is all about?

You see when a war is won they establish the balance of power, then they start cutting up, giving this to that one, this to that one, and the British are the slickest of all the Demons. I mean that British Devil is a Chief Devil. Yes they're the Devil, hell yes they're Devils! He's smart enough to make you think you're British. This one over here has got a lot to learn from that buddy over there now. That's the Master of Tricknology.

ONE WORLD GOVERNMENT

Look man, when they go to war they cut up, take a border from this one, give it to that one, take territory from one give it to another, knowing that at some future time the owner is going to claim what belongs to them, and the other is going to claim that "it was given to me at the Versailles Conference, it was given to me." So then here comes the international bankers again financing both sides in the conflict.

After World War I was over the manipulators knew it was only a matter of time before World War II would begin. They knew it wasn't a war to end all wars, it was just a cessation momentarily in the conflict. Then Hitler rose, Hitler rose wanting to get back the land that was taken from Germany in World War I. Many people who study history they don't know the manipulative forces that create the tensions that begin the War. They are never brought out into the frame. And the landscape painters, you guys in the press, you're really the landscape artists, you paint a picture for the gullible public.

The crash in 1929 was engineered, well orchestrated. They can set inflation, deflation, recession, boom, they can do it all scientifically. It's interesting that the stock market before the crash had reached dizzying heights, almost like it is right now. And then all of a sudden the Federal Reserve put on the brakes, after letting a lot of money out, it puts on the brakes and tightened the money. Tightened the discount rate on money. People had to sell, they called loans, people had to sell stocks in order to pay their debt. Stock market crashed, but the wise insiders had already prepared and made a boom while the majority of the stock holders went bust. I wonder if history will repeat itself, in a few days, we'll see.

After World War II America gets involved again, late. See, after World War I the international bankers, and these birds, they wanted a one world government. So through Woodrow Wilson again, they wanted to set up the League of Nations. You better sit there cool man and take notes. Yeah, school is out, that school, this one is in, and you'd probably learn more here today than you ever learned in your life, if you study political science, economics or religion.

Where was I? Yeah the League of Nations, and just as the table was set for America to come in, America backed out. The League of Nations died. But the international bankers really wanted to get America involved in this thing. World War II set up, got America in the war, borrowed a lot more money, international bankers happy, going to charge a lot of interest, income tax going up, and if you look at the FBI, and you look at the

ADL, and you look at the IRS, these are convenient tools. I can't say the FBI didn't get a few criminals, but when you are a criminal outfit yourself, when you see yourself as above the law though you are brought into existence by means of the law, then you become a criminal outfit chasing criminals.

CIA, it's a criminal outfit, killing Presidents and Kings and overthrowing governments, and causing tens of thousands and hundreds of thousands of innocent people to die because leaders would not play ball with the foreign policy objective of Europe and America. This is real man. This is Satan's world and you can't run out here with no pop gun in Satan's' world and think you going to do something.

The thing that Satan is most afraid of is truth. Now let's see what happens. After World War II was over Russia and America that had fought side by side to defeat the Germans, the Italians and the Japanese; but when the war was over a few days later, it was a cold war between the Russians, the Americans, the Communist, the Capitalist, the East and the West. And the root of Communism and the root of Capitalism is the same group of people. Did you hear me? Are you going to sleep? I said the root of Communism and the root of Capitalism is from the same group.

They started both philosophies, they financed both philosophies and when Russia was strong they said "Ah, now we have a balance of power." So Russia now is bringing people into her sphere of influence, China, many others under Karl Marx, Lenin, Trotsky, financed by wicked bankers many of whom were Jews. Now look man, I'm going to stop right here. See this old crap that you use called anti-Semitism, that's a smoke screen.

ANTI-WHITE

Look here, look here. Now I want you members of the press and you so-called scholars and religious leaders and teachers, think with me a minute. Are there some Black people that are no-good? Wait a minute, talk to me, are there some no-good Black people? Sure. And if I talk about some no-good Black people what Blackman has ever called me anti-Black? Wait, wait, wait, wait. If you listen to my lectures I take on the evil of our own self, beat it down and try to encourage righteousness where evil exists. Nobody calls me anti-Black.

Are white people sacred? Wait, wait now, listen, wait, wait, wait, I got to ask the question because some of you, some of you are a little slow in answering. I asked, "are white people sacred?" You're damn right they're not! Now look, if white people have done evil to the darker people of the world and somebody points it out, does that mean I'm anti-white? If you really want to see an anti-white person, stand a white person up and tell them look in the mirror. Because white people have done more to injure white people than any Black people on the Earth. So will the real anti-white man stand up.

You all had a thirty year war in Europe against yourselves. We weren't killing you, you were killing your dumb self. You had a hundred year war in Europe against yourself. We wasn't bothering you, we were busy killing ourselves. World War I was all you Europeans, fighting over who going to get rights and territories in Africa. So don't tell me nothing about anti-white, and then if I point out your evil all of a sudden I'm a racist. You just frightened of truth, just tell the truth. You don't mind writing it in your books, but don't let one of your ex-slaves read your book and then read you. "Now he's uppity."

Now wait, now how many of you were involved in the holocaust, raise your hand? You see what I'm saying. Weren't none of us involved man. We didn't kill one Jew, and if there were a holocaust today, damn it, you would not find most of these harming one hair on the head of a Jewish man, woman or child. And that's true. So if we were not involved there, we were not, just not involved. But that was your white brother, Hitler, aided by your white Jewish brothers, Warburg and Rothschild, Lord Milner and Schiff and Loeb and Kuhn. It's your brother.

Oh hell if they kill two million, one million, five million, six million we didn't have nothing to do with it. The Pope, that's your brother, though some of us call him father, but that was your brother, your white brother, he looked the other way. Pope didn't say nothing. Franklin Delano Roosevelt that's your white brother, he looked the other way. But when it came time to open those camps, those death camps, the first one to open it was a Black man. God damn it, how in the hell can you call us anti-Semitic in the face of your own damn evil to yourself and your own people.

I know you don't like my language, I don't like it either, but I'm angry as hell, you know that, and sometimes if I didn't cuss I'd kill. So you just might as well sit there and take it, I had to read that crap you put in the paper. You killed each other. Little Jews dying while big Jews made money. Little Jews being turned into soap while big Jews washed themselves with it. Jews playing violins, Jews playing music while other Jews marched into the gas chambers. We wasn't there, we had nothing to do with it.

Well, why all of a sudden am I anti-Semitic? Tell me, don't get frightened. Well if I scare you, then you know you just going to be scared then, because I'm not getting softer no time from now on. You looked for this. How did I get to be an anti-Semite? What have I done? You can't find one Jewish person that I have hurt. I've not cut nobody that's Jewish, fought nobody that's Jewish, what have I done?

I told the truth about Jewish involvement in the slave trade, your own writers say the same thing. Well if they're not anti-

Semitic for writing it, then how in the hell am I anti-Semitic for reading what they wrote and then saying it? Come on reason with me. I didn't write your history, you wrote it. And then the sad thing when you confront them with what their own scholars have said, they say 'Well, this is part of the old conspiracy talk,' but who's saying this, not the little Jews?

Let me read you something. Listen, this is on page forty-six of this little book 'None Dare Call It Conspiracy' by Gary Allen, which I'd like to get ten thousand copies of it and have everybody read it. If it is a lie I didn't tell it I'm just reading now. Thank you all for teaching me how to read. It says:

"One major reason for the historical black-out on the role of the international bankers in political history is that the Rothschilds were Jewish." Listen, "anti-Semites have played into the hands of the conspiracy by trying to portray the entire conspiracy as Jewish. Nothing could be further from the truth. The traditionally Anglo-Saxon J.P. Morgan and Rockefeller, international banking institutions, have played a key role in the conspiracy, but there is no denying the importance of the Rothschilds and their satellites. However, it is just as unreasonable and immoral to blame all Jews for the crimes of the Rothschilds as it is to hold all Baptists accountable for the crimes of the Rockefellers." Listen, "the Jewish members of the conspiracy have used an organisation called the Anti-Defamation League."

Oh, I'm going to read that one again, I got to slow down, because I want you to get this. "The Jewish members of the conspiracy." What conspiracy? The international banking conspiracy, have used an organisation called the Anti-Defamation League as an instrument to try to convince everyone that any mention of the Rothschild's, or their allies, is an attack on all Jews.

In this way they have stifled almost all honest scholarship on international bankers, and made the subject taboo within the University. Now let's go on, I'm still quoting. "Any individual, or book, exploring this subject is immediately attacked by hundreds of ADL communities all over the country. The ADL has never let truth or logic interfere with its highly professional smear jobs. When no evidence is apparent the ADL, which staunchly opposed so-called McCarthyism, accuses people of being latent anti-Semites."

READY FOR THE SLAUGHTER

Now, did you hear my Saviours Day lecture? Did you hear me condemn all Jews? I condemned the wicked ones. Are there wicked ones among the Jews? And they would be sometimes even more wicked because they got more Revelation. Come on! Guess what, right after that a full-page ad [appeared] in the New York Times, taken out by whom? ADL. Let me read what they say. This has proven my point. These are the watchdogs for the international bankers. They are the watchdogs for the secret government that manipulates Presidents and Congress.

I got to tell it man. Almost all your Black Congress men are honorary citizens, members of the Knesset, did you know that? Most Senators, Black and white, honorary members of the Knesset. You all do your homework and tell me how many there are. To hell, are you a honorary member of Ghana's parliament, any African governments parliament? Watchdogs attack dogs:

"Farrakhan attacks Jews, Catholics and others," listen to this. "The Nation of Islam has a well documented public record of racism and bigotry." You mean more than you? "And their abysmal track record continues, as recently as February 26 1995, Minister Louis Farrakhan railed against Jews at his annual Saviours Day message in Chicago, using centuries old conspiracy theories and code words like international bankers. Farrakhan excoriated Jews as those who have been at the root of the control of the banking system of the Federal Reserve."

See now, you never read nothing about my speech in the paper. Hey press, you were there, how come you didn't say nothing? Why didn't you say something about what I said? Because you know that subject is taboo. But now Jewish writers immediately attack me in the New York Times editorials. What are you afraid of? You're afraid that people will know the truth and go free. Well I think I can begin to close this.

The international bankers are waxing rich, have waxed rich in this East-West struggle. The Russians put the first Cosmonaut in space, Kennedy had to get his man up. The space program was put into existence. Where they get the money from to finance it? The debt kept growing, the debt kept growing. Russia developed this kind of jet plane, this kind of tank. They come before Congress and the Appropriations Committee for more and more money to develop more technology, more weapons. "We need more nuclear weapons," more this, more that, so the arms race, who did it enrich? The international bankers.

And when Russia collapsed, what was the first thing they agreed to do? Scrap some of their nuclear weapons. Who paid for it? Tax payers. Who's paying the interest on the debt of weapons systems, that you better not use? It's the tax payers. That's the kind of government that you live in. I ain't finished. Russia has collapsed leaving only America as a super power, but America, the greatest nation in the last six thousand years is all but taken from the people who claim to be citizens, and who believe in her promise. This country has just about been taken.

Oh, there's a Scripture in the Bible that reads like this, it is in Ezekiel, the twenty-first chapter, "Ah it is wrapped up and made bright and ready for the slaughter." America is already wrapped up. Who wrapped up this country? What is she wrapped up in? How did she get made ready for the slaughter? Well let me just point it out. You got a couple more minutes, I got, I got a few.

Did you know that there's been a carefully orchestrated scheme going on in this country to set the whole country up to break it down, so that it would become a part of a World government. Not the World Order that Bush is talking about, Bush was just promoting something that is in the interest of people of big, big money. Russia is already broken, now how are they going to break this country. Well she's really already broken. She's nearly $5 trillion in debt. You can't even imagine that kind of money.

The interest on the debt alone, is over $300 billion a year. You didn't hear me did you? Somebody getting fat off America. Somebody got control of the country and you can't even see that your elections are a sham. Who you voting for? Well we're voting for, it's either Clinton or Bush, or the other fellow, whoever can make a wave in their hair and put their hand in their pocket and sound like Kennedy. This is all show business, B.S. man. And the masses of the people are being manipulated to think that you voted for somebody to have supreme power. That man ain't in no supreme power position. Your government has been taken over already. Now let's see what part you play in this.

DESTRUCTION OF THE FAMILY

Forty years ago America had strong family. Forty years ago manufacturing was the bedrock of employment for the working people of America, and you would see the working man leave his home with a lunch pail going into the many factories of America making the shoes, the garments, the machinery that made America the greatest industrial power in the world.

At that time women were not in the work force, women were home. It ain't that home is your place, but the home is your base, and if you lose your base you've lost your place, and let me tell you something woman, I don't need no applause, I want you to listen. You're so busy trying to compete with men but you've lost your own maternal instincts. You've lost your own natural role as the shaper of the destiny of a people.

There was a time when women were more acclimated to the home, rearing the children, keeping their homes as places of refuge, and teaching the values of their religion and their culture to their children. But someone decided we must take the woman out of the home. Someone decided that women must no longer know home economics. There was a time when women knew how to cook. There was a time when women knew how to sew. There was a time when women knew how to do needlework and crochet. You say "Yeah, but I'm a doctor, and I'm a lawyer, and I'm a teacher." Yeah, but you're not a good mother. And who the hell cares if you're a good doctor, and a good lawyer, and a good stenographer, but your children have been cut loose from your own string.

You've lost your children Black woman, white woman, all by design. You don't cook no more, Sara Lee cooks for you. You don't cook no more, takes too much time to prepare health for your children. Now you pop it in the microwave and put it on the table. And where are your children? They're in the streets. The enemy has taken your children right out from under your own control, then put you in jail if you discipline them. Look at yourselves. They tell you, you are the parent, but they don't have to tell you when they go get an abortion in some places. They don't have to tell you that they got Norplant. They don't have to tell you that their taking the pill, but you're the mother. They have taken our babies from us. You the parent, you can't teach values any more, you're too busy, so television is now the teacher in your house.

And what is television teaching your babies? You come in anytime day or night, MTV is on, children rocking and rolling, chucking and jiving, stepping and dancing, their behinds twisting and shaking. You've lost your children. Your children are not looking to you as a mother for wisdom and guidance. They'll tell you what they saw on television "I saw Oprah's show and Oprah said," and "I saw so and so and they said!" You ain't got no more say so. They've taken over. This is not an accident, this is by design.

You ain't the man in your house no more, Satan is king in your house, he rules your wife and your children. Try and tell your wife "take that damn lipstick off." Try and tell her "hey baby, cover yourself." Try and make your daughters righteous, see what they will tell you. Put your children on television, they got dresses all the way up to their crotch, sitting down crossing their legs on television. "And what's wrong with the way I dress," because you couldn't pass on no culture, no value.

The country is destroyed. Drugs brought in. It ain't just Black folk using drugs, white folk using it, children using it. Well, mother no longer at home to see after the rearing of her children, many fathers put out of work, factories closed, mothers left to rear the children by themselves, and since many mothers had to go to work, children reared by television and the controlling influence of television started gradually to deteriorate to a sex-centred entertainment centre.

We all got a sex drive, every one in here is driven by that urge. But my God, if everything you hear is "I want to freak you," your own Black woman on television with a string in her behind, showing yourself in a most disgraceful way. How are you going to have your children look at this and then you tell them that's indecent, when it's on television?

Television has gone all the way down, newspapers all the way down, recordings all the way down. Our great talent is being used to make us purveyors of a culture of filth and degeneracy all over the world. Look at your self, you're human pigs. Oh I'm going to say it again. I said look at your self. You have become human swine. You love filth, and the more low down and dirty the thing is, the more you like it.

How is homosexuality growing so, till you can't even have a slumber party because little girls are having sex with little girls, and little boys having sex with little boys. Old men finding little boys to play with, old women finding little girls to play with, and it's alright to you now. When I was coming along, if you were a homosexual you had to hide it, because that was unacceptable behaviour in any community where religion, and the teaching and precepts of God were taught. Now listen, wait a minute. Now you are going to call me a homosexual basher, and I am not going for that. I am not going for that.

A homosexual brother and sister, that's my Brother, my Sister and I love them. Okay. Yeah I love them. Some are very beautiful people, here. The way of life is distorted, "by whose standard?" God's. Now look man, wait a minute, wait a minute. Don't have to applaud. Homosexuality has to be looked at as well as adultery, fornication and all of the freakishness that we are involved in. Pastors what the hell is wrong with you? You do not want to talk about it anymore. Why? Because many pastors are homosexual. Wait a minute, wait a minute man. School is in, school is in man. The Holy Qur'an refers to homosexuality as an abomination, meaning it is so utterly loathsome in the sight of God that "A man would go to another man with lust in his heart as he should be going to a female." I hope I ain't hurt no feelings, but it's better for me to talk to you.

Homosexuality is being encouraged, its being promoted. One day soon I am going to take a subject on it, not homosexual bashing but just to talk about it, how does it happen? There are so many forces at work in society to turn a young man out or a young woman out. You just can't tell somebody who's homosexual, "Well homosexuality is wrong." Well yeah, but what are they going to do about the forces that made them that? How do they get straight to combat that?

All sin has to be engaged in struggle, all of it, not some of it, all of it. There ain't none of us so holy that we can look down on somebody else who has a particular ailment that is different from our ailment. But all of us are sick and all of us must engage sin until we overcome it. But how? That's a subject for another time.

And you look at the kind of people who are promoting girly magazines. See that's why I want to say to those who are Jews - see, you want us to take our own to task, that's why when Farrakhan speaks you go to every Black leader you can and you say to them "Isn't there anything you can say about Farrakhan?" Well I'm asking you ain't there something, damn it, that you can say about them damn freaks in Hollywood, that are your own kin, your own kith that claim to be Jews. Talk to me I want to hear from you.

You want Black people to attack me because you say I'm a racist. The Jews have had the prophets of God and you know what is right and you know what is wrong, but you won't lift your voice against your own brothers who are making themselves wealthy off of the weakness and ignorance of the people.

Why don't you call your Hugh Heffner into question? Why don't you call David Geffin into question? Am I wrong? Tell me. You want my Black brothers to call me into question, well where is the guts in the Jewish community? Where is the righteousness in that community that you won't even condemn your own criminals, Milensky?

Many of the criminals, the Italian criminals, put money in the Catholic church. Tell me I am a liar. Damn it, but if I know you have got dope money, I won't take your money. I don't need a whore's money and if I know you're whoring you can't give me a damn dime. You don't come to me saying "I made a killing of the numbers" and I take your money, keep your damn money! I'll get mine, but I'll get mine by following righteousness.

I said if I know, if I know that you are dealing I can not deal with you until you straightened up, because it is only honest money, money earned from righteous endeavours that should be used to build the kingdom of God. And so dear family I want to close. I hope you don't think so hard of me, but if you do it's alright.

America is going down. They have destroyed the educational system, it's gone, it's gone man. When I went to school by the time I was fifteen and sixteen years old I had at least four years of Latin, two years of German, two years of Spanish, one year of French. I had medieval history, ancient history, American history and modern history. I had algebra, geometry; solid and plain. I had trigonometry and calculus, algebra; one and two, before I left high school.

When I went to college I did not have to buy a book because I knew everything that they were teaching because of the background I had in the Boston public school system. Everybody in my class even the dumbest knew how to read. How come America is turning out 30% functional illiterates today? You graduating from school and can't read. That's not an accident that's by design man, because if you can't read how will you ever know what's hidden and written in books. Then if you can't read you get your world view from television. You get your world view from those who are the mind manipulators and you become one of the gullible mass of the people, the eighty five per cent who believe in a mystery God.

SILVER CERTIFICATE

And so beloved in my conclusion, the "dollar" is all but gone. This "dollar" used to be called the "silver certificate." Everything over five dollars at a certain point was backed by gold and silver, backed it all the way up. But in 1933 America went off the gold standard and the dollar wasn't backed by gold anymore. And some time thereafter it went off the silver standard and all silver certificates were pulled in and a federal reserve note was handed out.

When I was a little boy you could get a dollar and it would say "Pay to the bearer on demand a dollar in silver." Today you can't go nowhere and get any real value back for this because it's not backed by silver or gold. Now, The Honourable Elijah Muhammad in his book "Message to the Blackman in America," said "America's great wealth, her dollar is now fallen to pieces." He said that "whoever took America off of the gold and silver standard, when that was done America's financial doom was sealed."

"At the time of writing the English Pound Sterling had lost fifty percent of its value and America's dollar has lost everything now as power backing for her currency. Today the currency of America is not backed by any sound value, silver or gold. The note today is something that the government declares it will give you the value in return, but does not name that value, but they are not backing this currency anymore with silver or with gold. Well what should we expect in the very near future under the fall of America's dollar? This could mean that we would have a 100% inflation, well what could happen under a hundred percent inflation?" The hand of God is against America's wealth.

Oh the wealthy bankers, now they're worried because their world is coming down. I heard The Honourable Elijah Muhammad say "that one day that you would see the wealthy take a thousand dollar bill and light their cigars with it because it would be worthless." In the future while this has some degree of power we ought to put as much paper as we can together and take this paper and go and buy as much land as we can get our hands on. Because the real value is not paper money, the real value is land. And when the dollar, when the dollar won't spend, the land will produce if you have got seed and a healthy rain and sunshine, you will eat.

But oh my brothers and sisters, if you look in the book of Daniel it talks about that great image with a golden head, a breast plate of silver and feet and legs of iron and miry clay.

Daniel saw that vision or Nebuchadnezzar saw it, he didn't understand it, couldn't handle it. He was going to kill people who didn't understand or couldn't tell him, not only tell him what he saw but tell him what it meant. So they came to Daniel and Daniel began to pray to God because he said only God knew the meaning of this. And as Daniel prayed God began to reveal its meaning.

Well my friends, The Honourable Elijah Muhammad broke it down and I'll just tell you a little of what he said. In the vision of Daniel the images head is gold which represents the standard metal of worship. And the placing of this metal at the head and not at the feet gives us again a chance at the meaning and significance of Daniel's vision. The head of gold and the breast of silver represents the two countries, England and her sterling, and America and her gold. England's sterling pound and America's $11 billion or more dollars in gold made these two countries the head of the nations of the earth.

This was because their great wealth of money, gold and silver which they hoped to use to sway the nations to bow down to their bidding. But the fall of this great god of gold and silver and the manoeuvring of power to be the instrument that caused the fall of the great statute of gold and silver held by England and America, has come from Divine power and not from the nations' power.

America and England built up their silver and the gold from the poor. As you build up the statue you start from the feet and the legs. The feet are iron mixed with miry clay, it's telling you there's weakness in the support. Gold is a heavy metal and if you have ever seen a water-head baby, a baby with a big unusual head that weighs so much more than the body can grow to support, then anything that hits that leg will tumble that head. And this is why the ADL, the FBI, the IRS and the federal government use their power against anybody who can speak to the masses and cause the masses to listen. Because anybody that empowers the masses shakes the leg, and the head of gold will come tumbling down.

England, that said the sun never set on her empire, now the sun can't find her empire. America, America had $11 billion in gold, now its down to about $1 billion. France began to make America pay her in gold. Now America's [dollar] has no value. Did you see how shaky it got when the dollar fell last week to an all time low? You ain't looking brothers and sisters but the country is in trouble. America is in trouble. Clinton is in trouble. You and I are in trouble and the only way to get out, is to come on to God. Submit yourself to God, follow the Guidance and the Wisdom of God and when you follow the Guidance and Wisdom of God you will know what to do with dollars, but we have got to do it quick.

JACOB TO ISRAEL

Stock market may crash, it's at a dizzying height over four thousand, and they're manipulating it right now, but all is well with the righteous. I would like to close with these words. To all of you who are looking by satellite, all of you who are listening, Israel was named, or the name given to Jacob after he wrestled with the angel all night long. God changed his name from Jacob to Israel. Jacob the supplanter became the Israel who prevailed with God. Old Israel prevailed but prevailed because God allowed it, God allowed America to wax strong. God allowed America to become the greatest nation in the last six thousand years. God allowed communism to come up, God allowed it all to happen.

But now there is a new Israel, you may not want to believe it, but the God that I represent is the same God you read about in the Old Testament, that was the God of a nation and that he threatened to kill all the enemies of Israel. Not that Israel in the Middle East, but the Israel that it is talking about is called the Nation of Islam in the West. I know you are plotting against us, but I want to tell you what my God is poised to do for you.

Within the next thirty days I want you to look at the natural calamities that our God will bring because of your evil plans against His Nation. I don't care who don't like the Nation of Islam, the God of the Nation, a Living Man, a Human Being, Master Fard Muhammad, take it or let it alone. He is the Lord God of Israel.   Just leave it alone if you can't handle it. But I am telling you, our God can't wait for you to make your move. I am in America as a dare. He dares you to touch me. Come on if you want to die. Come on government of America, do what you've got to do, so that the God of the Nation of Islam, that you have thought was the Jews of yesterday. Remember your Bible Christian "the Jew is not the Jew outwardly, but the Jew is the Jew inwardly by the circumcision of the heart."

All of these wicked ones who have given Judaism a bad name, they are members of the synagogue of Satan. And unless the righteous Jews condemn and cast out the wicked Jews then all will partake of the Wrath of God. I warn you in the name of Allah, leave us alone, your time is just about up. The last six in the number of the beast, which is the number of a man, six hundred three score and six. The last six represents sixty years of grace.

I'm at the end. If the scholars say that the world of Satan ended in 1914, sixty years from 1914 brings you to 1974.   A lot happened in 1974. The whole nature of the climate changed. But you marked your calendar wrong because grace had not come in 1914. God had to extend you His grace. He came in 1930 and it took Him three and a half years to prepare "Grace" and He put "Grace" in the midst of you America.   Not a white man, but a Blackman from Georgia, he's your grace. He showed you your evil but he gave you a way out, that if you repented and did right by the children of God; the new nation of Israel, one who would prevail with God who is here to supplant your world, if you would do right by us, God will give you an extension of time.

Elijah Muhammad started his mission free of Master Fard Muhammad in 1934, now you mark sixty years from there. He said "sixty, you would get no more than seventy years of grace." So here we are, 1994 marked the end of grace and you are in the last ten years of your power. Now you are looking at Europe a boiling cauldron. Oh America it's going to break out into war over there, but this time the international bankers are not going to prosper. Because when Master Fard Muhammad was six years old he came into the knowledge of what his mission was. As Yakub at the age of six came into the knowledge of his mission, Master Fard saw Himself pushing the Rockefellers, the Dupont's, the J.P. Morgan's, the Warburg's, the Schiff's the Vanderlip's - He saw himself pushing them into a lake of fire.

This is the end of your world Satan, we locked in this struggle. I know you think you are going to win, but Satan your stuff is finished, your game is over. Now between here and 2004 this is the end of your time. America can survive or America will die like Egypt, Babylon, Rome, Sodom and Gomorra and all the other wicked kingdoms of the past. You can take it or let it alone. You don't have no redemption power left. You wicked and adulteress generation that seeketh after a sign. There is no sign for you but the sign of Jonah. As Jonah was in the belly of the whale three days and three nights so shall the Son of Man be in the heart of the earth.

And now we have come to you like Jonah went to Nineveh, and unless you put on sack cloth and ashes and repent of your evil, America you are finished; finished as a power in the world, finished as a great nation and it will be your own leaders who led you down the path of hell and destruction. And this is why I am calling for a march on Washington, a march on Washington, because Blackman you are the new Jonah who has been in the belly of this whale for over three hundred years.

Now if you stand up and repent for not taking your responsibility as a man and a servant of God, if you will atone for your evil of putting your woman out to fight for you while you did nothing, you Blackman have been a disgrace, but God is calling on you to turn around and take your responsibility. But you have got to repent and you've got to clean up and go into Washington, like Jonah going to Nineveh.

We are going to call on America in a Day of Atonement, a real Day of Atonement to atone for your evils to the native American, atone for your evil to our fathers and mothers, atone for your evils to the poor, atone for the wickedness of your mis-guided leadership, and repent. "And if you my people who are called by my name will turn from your wicked ways, humble yourself and pray, then," not before, "then will I hear from heaven and heal your land."

I am from Elijah Muhammad, I am "Grace" to you America and I am Grace to you Blackman and Black woman. God will give you grace if you hearken to the voice of One who is grace, in your midst. God will give you grace America if you recognise that I am telling the truth; which you already know, and if you recognise that you can't solve your problems. But God can solve your problems, if you let Him. But if you try to kill "Grace," I ain't talking about daddy grace, I have never claimed nothing for myself and I don't have to, my work speaks for me - but I am grace to you. But if you try to harm me, if you do like that dragon in Revelations who stood before the woman and spewed out of its mouth a flood to carry the woman away in the flood, because she feared - the dragon feared that a new boy was coming up that would rule the nations with a rod of iron.

You can't stop this, but if you would act wise toward it - God, He will have mercy on you. And like He gave Nineveh two hundred years of extended time, maybe you can get the same. But I kind of think you've gone a little crazy. I kind of think you are going to do everything you can to kill me this year. I kind of think you've really lost it. I'm going to be here if God pleases. You do what you think you have to do, but I am warning you when you see your cities tumbling down on you, when you see death everywhere, remember what I told you, you brought it on yourself.

The righteous, seek refuge in God. There is no place for you to hide nor them except in God. Take away to God, find His bosom and stay there. I believe I have found His bosom and yeah, though I walk through the valley of the shadow of death I don't fear any evil, because I know that God is with me.

QUIBILLAH SHABAZZ

And so as I leave you, on behalf of Quibillah Shabazz and on behalf of the Shabazz family, I am asking all of us to stand up for Quibillah. I'm asking all of us to recognise what the FBI has done. They manipulated the daughter of Malcolm X, they manipulated the murder of the father and now they want to manipulate the daughter, to go to prison for supposedly paying somebody $250 as a down-payment to kill me.

The government has agreed from what I understand, to drop the charges if Quibillah will permit herself to be sent to a mental institution for forty-five days and then after she comes out another forty-five days, they have something else for her to do. She must sign a paper saying that she will not ever use the word entrapment, that she was entrapped, and she must apologise to the government of the United States. Now brothers and sisters that's as low down as you can get. The US attorney who is handling that is David Lillehaug. I hope that address is coming up on the screen. Mr Lillehaug, I hope Mr Lilliehaug I am saying your name right. But everyone who is here and everyone who is listening take this address down:

David Lilliehaug, what is the address, is it on the screen? What is it? Why don't you bring it to me since everybody has got it. Mr David Lilliehaug, US attorney, District of Minnesota,

243 US Court House, 110 South Fourth Street, Minneapolis, Minnesota, 55401. Now don't get discouraged that's a lot of writing. But if you don't want to write a letter just get a postcard and all you have got to say is "set Quibillah Shabazz free with no strings attached," or anything else you might want to write. I mean no, no, no nothing like that. Then you ought to write a letter to the Attorney General, Janet Reno.

Janet Reno, Attorney General, US Department of Justice, Canton and Constitution Avenue North West, Washington DC, 20530. Everyone of you should have been given this when you came in. Well now, I want you to promise me, I know we don't write but I want you to write this time. We want to amass public opinion to make the world see that something is wrong with the justice system.

You know this man Fitzpatrick or Sumer's was a member of the JDL which is akin to the ADL. And he is on the payrole of the FBI, see how they all hang out together. I think that all Black organisations should make up their minds that we will not talk to the ADL. We will have nothing to do with that gangster group that has spied on Martin Luther King Junior, spied on his father, spied on Black people, turned over our files to the governments in South Africa, worked with the FBI to destroy Black leadership while at the same time they put on a face to say that they are fighting against anti-Semitism.

Well let's leave them alone, in the sense that none of us as Black leaders, none of us as Black organisations should take a dime from them. And if you are really representing your people, your own people will support you. How many of you will write that letter? Is that a promise? Is your word bond? I am going to write mine but I am not going to write a postcard. I am supposed to be the one that was to be killed.

And if you think it's a surprise that I am defending my sister, you know we can never bring back and really right the wrongs of thirty years ago. There is nothing we can do. Thirty years ago is thirty years ago, but we don't have to allow the evil of yesterday to corrupt today. Quibillah Shabazz and the whole Shabazz family, my sons and daughters, The Honourable Elijah Muhammad's sons and daughters, Martin Luther King's sons and daughters, Jesse Jackson's sons and daughters, they should be the vanguard of a new era for Black people. Free of the scars of thirty years ago, free of the pain that each of us have suffered, free of the mistake and the errors that we have made in struggling for the justice of our people. Let the children go free.

So I say to Dr. Betty Shabazz, that we in the Nation will stand with her and her children and will do everything in our power to see that, that Sister Quibillah Shabazz goes free. Will you help us to do that?

Thank you and may Allah bless you all, as I greet you in peace.

As-Salaam-Alaikum.

1st April   1995

The Conspiracy
of the International Bankers

In the Name of Allah the Beneficent the Merciful
who came in the person of Master Fard
Muhammad, the Great Mahdi. We thank Him
for His coming and for His raising up in our
midst a Divine Leader, Teacher and Guide, our
Messenger The Most Honourable Elijah
Muhammad. I greet all of you my dear brothers
and sisters of Springfield Massachusetts and
other places in the greeting words of peace.
We say it in the Arabic language As-Salaam-
Alaikum.

To Minister Yusuf Muhammad, to the Labourers and staff of Mosque number thirteen and to all of the wonderful believers who worked so hard not only to prepare this night for us but to open a very beautiful mosque and shopping plaza here in the city of Springfield as a sign that we are determined to do something for ourselves.

To the Ministers of The Honourable Elijah Muhammad, community leaders of Springfield and to all of you I am very honoured to have this privilege to come back to Springfield. Springfield is one of those wonderful cities that I have so many fond memories of during my early days in the study of the teachings of Islam under the leadership of The Honourable Elijah Muhammad. I used to come in and out of Springfield quite regularly. It has grown tremendously since those days.

DEBT BURDEN

But now let us get right to our business. America as we speak is in deep trouble. She is burdened with tremendous debt and as in any family when a husband and wife are burdened with debt, that kind of stress begins to undermine the internal workings of the house. If that is so as individuals, it is equally so with a nation.   When a nation has the kind of debt that America has, nearly $5 trillion in public debt, with the closing down of factories and their moving out of America into third world countries because of the cheap labour market, and more and more Americans out of work, over 10 million and steadily growing, then this overwhelming pressure on the society causes social disorganisation.   The disruption of family and all of the tensions in the society that could be hidden under good times become manifest when times get tough.

Black people in general suffer more when there is a downturn in the economic picture of this country, and when tensions rise socially in the country. There is always this need it appears, to suppress and oppress in even greater dimensions the Black population. In this case Black men are more vulnerable than any other member of the society because as Black men we have borne the brunt of America's hatred for Black people. And there seems to be a great fear of retribution on the part of whites that Black people one day will attempt to pay them back for the evils that their fathers, and now even some of the children of those fathers, continue to do to Black people.

To hear Newt Gingrich and Senator Dole and the Republicans talk about cutting back welfare as though we have been the burden on the society. To talk about welfare reform is one thing but to talk about the removal of a safety net on families that need help, that is cold and heartless. To cut back programs that are necessary to get young people moving in a proper direction, to make young people, and poor people, and the elderly suffer for government mismanagement of resources is wicked. The social unrest that is already in the country, the seeds of revolution, are being fed by social and political conditions that make us wonder is somebody really trying to destroy this nation and scapegoating Black and poor people for their wicked agenda? I would like to take a few minutes; in a very, I would call it a fire side chat, to deal with these kinds of issues.

The people in Congress who make laws are not from the poor. Most of your Congress persons are members of the rich and wealthy class of American people. Those who genuinely can advocate for the poor are overwhelmed by the business of the rich. So the poor in America, Black and white, Hispanic, Native American, Asian and otherwise, really do not have strong advocacy. Listen now, Jesus said "Blessed are the poor." Well, I know he told the truth, but we have to ask ourselves, how is any poor man blessed being poor? When you wake up in the morning with insufficient food to feed your children, insufficient money to pay the rent, or living under a bridge, or in a card board box, and you are a veteran who fought for America, how could you feel in that condition; blessed?

As I studied that scripture I said Oh I see, the poor are blessed because Jesus came from the poor to be the advocate of the poor, and that's what got him in trouble with the rich, who were the bloodsuckers of the poor. Now, welfare is not the problem, head-start is not the problem, entitlement programmes that help young people go to college is not the problem. What is the real problem? And who is the real problem? Because you can not have a "what" if you don't have a "who," and if you know what the problem is and you don't know who is producing the problem then you are still at a loss. But when you know who, and you know what, and you know why, and you know when, and you know how, then, you may be able to get out of that problem. And so to scapegoat the poor and to make poor people the burden, when in fact the country was built on the backs of the poor.

The poor have always been the labour that made the country great. The poor slave made the South rich. The poor worker made the industrial north rich. The riches of the country have been gained on the backs of the poor, but now the poor are being looked at as an unnecessary population. Whether you are Black or white, Asian or Hispanic there is a movement to get rid of, not thousands, but millions of poor people not only in America, but throughout the world.

STANDARDS DESTROYED

Those of you who have lived sixty, seventy, eighty years you have never seen the health condition of the country worse than it is now. Here is America the most technologically advanced nation in the world, but the sickest, a population full of sick people, overweight people, diseased people. You that are elderly, that lived in the South when we did not have as much knowledge as we have today, as much science or technology as we have today, yet you lived longer and did better. But now cancer is eating up the American people Black and white.

High blood pressure, hypertension, cirrhosis of the liver, heart disease, not to mention the social diseases; gonorrhea, syphilis, herpes, AIDS and other viruses that are on the horizon that make AIDS look comfortable.

We just saw on the news in Japan somebody got on a subway and released in the air, a gas, some kind of phial filled with some kind of biological or chemical warfare, death and destruction. We have read that they are working on ethnic weapons. What is an ethnic weapon? You say we are all the same, in some sense we are. But how could they if we are all the same, find a bone and tell you that is the bone of an Asian, or a Black person, or a white person and the bone is thousands of years old, if we are all the same, then what science are they using to determine who this bone belongs to?

According to something that I read they are developing ethnic weapons that can ill-effect Blacks, and whites could be in the room and not be affected. I said "now that is interesting." Now here we are as Black people, some of us have never been homosexual dying of AIDS. Where did it come from? Who is responsible for it? What is happening to you, to us, to the country? I'm looking at mature men and women who forty years ago saw some sense of family and community, now family is gone, community is gone, no one seems to want to take responsibility for community.

The educational system is destroyed. When you send your children to school and I know, as a sports figure some of you say "stay in school," that's like saying to the convict stay in jail. It's almost that bad. Why should they stay in a place that they are being killed in? And I am not talking about guns, I'm talking about what's happening to the heads of our children.

Do you think this is accidental or do you think this has some design to it? How could I go to school fifty years ago, or more, up the street in Boston and come out of high school having four years of Latin under my belt, two years of German, two years of French, one year of Spanish, plane geometry, solid geometry, trigonometry, calculus, ancient history, medieval history, modern history. How could I come out knowing how to read, and the dumbest brother in the class knew how to read, and today America is graduating from ten to thirty per cent of her youth as functional illiterates? What's going on? What's going on? Marvin Gaye raised the question "What's going on?"

There was a time sisters when codes of decency said that even when you took off your clothes to go swimming you had something covering you. Today you are less covered than the lower animals. They have a tail to cover their sensitive parts and you walk with a string in your tail. What's going on?

There was a time when a man liked another man he had to keep that quiet, real quiet. He had to act like he could lift pianos with his hand. But today little children are performing sex acts that grown-ups who are older never even thought of. What's going on? What's going on? There was a time when children respected elders. There was a time when children listened to their parents, but today children have been moved beyond your grasp. You can't reach your own children, somebody else has more influence over your children than you have, and government is making it easier for children to disrespect the parents. You send them to school and the school teacher tells them to get condoms. You send your girls to school and somebody is teaching them about birth control and then some of your babies can go and have abortions and you the mother don't know anything about it.

You say "America the beautiful," I don't know about that. She is getting uglier everyday and somebody has to take responsibility for the ugliness of a nation, and it is not Louis Farrakhan. I did not do this. When we look and see the destruction of the educational system, and the destruction of home; family where marriage is no longer sacred, the vows that we take mean nothing. Where yesterday a man might think twice before interfering in another man's house, today it is not even a thought. Where yesterday a man might think twice before interfering with another man's daughter, today that is not even a consideration.

You say, "well things are changing," they really are. But God has given all of us a "standard" by which human behaviour is measured. When you obliterate and destroy the standard then what you think is moral, or I think is moral, becomes the standard. But you are not to determine the standard. You are not the author of the life that you have, so He who is the author of life, and the giver of life, and the designer of this life should be the one to set the standard. And how dare you psychologists, sociologists with your little scholarship, now want to pit your few years on the earth against the infinite wisdom of Him who is ageless.

The children are beyond the reach of teachers, the children are beyond the reach of parents and they're beyond the reach of preachers. Well, what happened, who put them beyond your reach? How did that go down and you do not even know what happened? How did they change the educational system on you and you were not even aware that the system was been radically altered to produce the madness that you are looking at?

You say, "Oh, no the school is not responsible for this." Yes, yes! Education is now a form of manipulation. You are not educated people. If you were properly educated that would be reflected in the society. If you had the knowledge that you think you have, then why can't you correct the problems your education says you are trained to correct? You're a sociologist but you can't correct the social problem. You're an economist and you cannot correct the economic problem. You're a psychiatrist and the people are going crazy all around you, and you are nuts yourself. You are a doctor and you are sick. Something's going on.

Hollywood, we used to be able to go the movies when I was a youngster. We saw some horror movies which would scare you half out of your wits, but love scenes were modest and if sex were involved you did not see it, you just got the hint something was going on. They had the moon come up or a rush of water, birds singing, and you would say "Oh, oh, I see." Do you remember? Today nothing is left to the imagination. If you are a decent parent you do not know what movie to see. "PG" I do not know what "PG" means. "Poor Girl." I used to think that getting an "X" meant that you were in the Nation. "Let me go and see this Muslim movie here, so and so 3X." Well just a little light humour. Hollywood is shaping attitudes. Hollywood is shaping attitudes towards homosexuality that are in direct conflict with the standard given by God. Hollywood is reshaping our values, moral values, and nobody is saying anything about that.

Now brothers and sisters, in the midst of all of this madness is a country that is dying from an internal rot, while the people watch Michael Jordan with his magnificent magic with a ball, or Shakeel or Dominic. They're getting ready to look at Brother Michael Tyson or Michael Jackson and this is fantastic magic, using the gifts of God to keep you busy doing nothing, while your world is being moved out from under you and you are partying your life away, smoking and drinking, laughing and dancing and the world is coming down around you. And the biggest hype of all is saved for religion.

Now if our brother preachers, sister preachers are in the audience, you have to ask yourself, are you really, really a disciple of Christ? Are you really that? I want to put something on your mind tonight. Now I know, I know that that is what we want to be. I did not ask you, do you want to be a disciple of Christ, I asked you, are you? "Oh, what you are questioning me for? Of course I am." But the reason I raised the question is because, if you in your life, don't have the power to overcome evil in your life, you are not really a disciple of Christ. I'm going to say that again. If you are powerless to deal with any form of sin you're not a disciple. Because the least disciple of Christ, got power to overcome evil in his or her own life. But more than that, if you are any kind of disciple of Christ, you have power to overcome evil wherever you shine the light of God's truth.

My question is, if in fact America is a Christian nation then where is Christ in government, in Congress, in the State legislature? Where is He in the city halls, in the police department, in the business ethics of the people? He is not there. You can't be a liar and a thief, and a cheat in Jesus' name. You can't be involved in "red lining" and be a disciple of Jesus Christ. You can't promote homosexuality and immorality and filth and be a disciple of Jesus Christ. Talk to me. This country is using Jesus' name as a shield for immoral, unlawful and wicked practice.

Now, religion is weak and powerless in the society. Oh, they invite you preachers to political gatherings "would you give the benediction we will have the benediction by reverend [so and so], we will have the convocation by reverend so and so. And after you say your few little words you get out of the way "and we are going to get down and take care of business." Men of God are relegated to little insignificant places except on Sunday. And I watch us on Sunday in front of our congregation acting like we are the powerful words to bring Revelation from God and inside the church hell is raging. And outside the church hell is raging, and we the men of God don't have no power to change the condition of our own society, our own communities. I ask you, what's going on? Well let me tell you, since I've asked the question.

ENVY DESTROYS THE ENVIER

You vote for a President and you think he's the man in power. Poor Bill Clinton. All these people that you think have real power that are seen and there is some unseen forces that are known by a few, but the masses don't know who is pulling the strings. How could Bill Clinton be the sole power, voted for by the American people to do the will of the American people, and Congress and the American people say don't bail out the Mexican peso - but Mr Clinton unilaterally gave $20 billion, but Americans are sleeping under bridges? Do you hear what I am saying? How did that happen? Why didn't' Dole say something? Why didn't Gingrich say something since they opposed it? What happened to their mouth? The American people don't know what is going on in this country. The country is going to hell. It's not Black people sending it there. We are the victims of what is going on. You didn't, I didn't know, but those who study Constitution know that only Congress has the right to print money, the instruments of credit.

The founding fathers of this nation who were slave holders, knew from European history that to take control of the central bank of a nation would be to seize control of the power of that nation, and then to direct the policies of that nation. So when the founding fathers got away from Europe and got away from the madness of Europe, they wanted to set America up on a firmer foundation. They didn't see us as being germane to that firm foundation. They didn't see Black people, Hispanic people, Native Americans, as ever becoming citizens of this house.

This was a house of white people, by white people, and for some white people, of some white people, by some white people, for some white people. It wasn't even for all white people. Thomas Jefferson and these persons knew that to see the central bank of the country go out of the grasp of the legitimate government of the people, would be worse than facing standing armies. Because, when you face a standing army you face an enemy that you can see. But when somebody is controlling your finances and got power to deflate the money, inflate the money, got power to create a downturn or an upswing at their whim send the stock market up or down, increase interest or decrease it and you can't say nothing, then power is not in your hands. So to give you the right to vote for somebody that is not the real power is a hypocrisy, is a deception, is Satanic.

Black people are not the problem, we're a part of the problem, but we are not the core of it. And to make the whole world look at you and me as [though] we're the ones who are undermining America; for our brothers in Japan to say "well, it is you know, the illiterate Negroes that are bringing the country down." For our Hollywood Black people to put a movie out, that demonstrates the darkest side of our own life, and whites who distribute these films put it all over the world, but not as the darkest side of us, but us. So that the world sees the problem in America, as some gang banging, dope selling, crack using Black people. So that when they start killing Black people wholesale, nobody cares.

It is the same way that when they kill nazi's, who cares? When they kill communists, who cares? When they kill so-called gooks, who cares? Well now, you are the nazi, the gook, the unwanted element all over the world. It is Black people that are unloved, unwanted and now the dye is set to kill Black people wholesale, and we are contributing to our own destruction by not waking up to see what is going on around us. And here I am, just one man with truth in my mouth and love of God, and love of you in my heart and as I rise up to tell the truth, America says "He's a hater, he's a bigot, he's an anti-Semite, don't listen to him."

Now I want to say this publicly; I know the press is probably gone, you have a deadline. Television you got the first few minutes and you know you will put that on the eleven o'clock news probably. But look brothers and sisters I would be unfit as a human being to hate somebody because they are Jewish, I want you to hear me. I would be unfit to be a member of the human family if I hated somebody because their skin colour was different from mine. It's not your physical characteristics that is the problem, it's the way that you think and the deeds that are done.

Now I said something, I said something in my Saviours Day lecture that I want to repeat because I want us to understand something about the workings of God and what "Revelation" really is. When God sends a prophet into the world, that prophet brings what is called "Revelation." Revelation reveals the unseen and the unknown. You cannot call it Revelation if you can find it in the library. Revelation is that which no scholar or no scientist knew of knowledge before. So when God sends a prophet to open up the unseen and the unknown, God then is moving human beings up toward him. Do you understand?

Now, to the members of the Jewish family who are present, look how blessed you are. You are a blessed people because God sent you more prophets, according to the Bible. The whole Old Testament represents prophet after prophet, after prophet coming to who? Israel.

But wait now. If the prophet comes and brings you Revelation, that is putting you in potential leadership in every field of human endeavour. Other people can be envious, but envy destroys the envier. You still can't stop Jewish people from the brilliant manifestation of their gifts by being envious and hateful. The record of the Jewish people and their accomplishments is before the world. You can envy them, you can hate them, you can speak evil of them, but you can not deny the undeniable, indisputable fact that they [are] at the head of every field of human endeavour.

Now that you that are here, if you are a lawyer, you go into the legal profession you have got to run into Jewish people at the top of it, that's not anti-Semitism that it is a fact. Doctor, are you a Doctor? At the top of that, Jewish people. If you are in research, science, at the top of it, Jewish people. If you are in the arts, Jewish people. If you are in business, Jewish people. Wherever you are, they are at the top. God made it that way. That's not hate. Now, if your wisdom is used in accordance with the moral standard of God and the prophets then you go up, and you take humanity up with you. But every time a prophet comes into the world he not only opens up the way for man to make an ascent to God, he also opens up the ways of descent to the bottomless pits of hell. Now, now, now let us deal with truth.

See you don't know who you are until wisdom comes to you. You may think you are a good person. "Oh, I'm a good person," You see all dumb people can say "I'm good." You can't do evil too much, you just too dumb to do too much. You can do your little madness and we understand that. That's child-like immature behaviour of an ignorant wicked doer. But hell, when knowledge comes to you, now if you couple knowledge with moral correctness then you become an agent of God. But if you take the wisdom and deny the moral standard then you become an agent of Satan, or Satan himself.

MANIPULATION OF MONEY

Now, listen, listen, listen, are you alright? Are you sure now? Now, just as there are Jews who received Revelation and held onto the moral standard and ascended in their manifestation of greatness and power, there is no doubt that there are others who rejected the moral standard but accepted the wisdom and became not the synagogue of the righteous, but partakers and members of the synagogue of Satan. Now, let us see what I am talking about. You will never after tonight open your mouth and call me an anti-Semite, because I am going to give you a definition of that term.

In Europe a man by the name of Rothschild, who claimed to be Jewish made this statement. "He really did not care who was king or ruler as long as he controlled the finance." Rothschild had five sons and he sent those sons into different parts of Europe. He sent one son to England, one to France, one to Italy, one to Austria and one stayed at home with the father in Germany, and they all became a part of the House of Rothschild.

But through manipulation of money, the son in England grew up and that became the Bank of England, the Bank of France, the Bank of Italy, the Bank of Austria, the Bank of Germany. These were central banks that printed the money of these nations, that now were in the hands of a family that had spread out with not the intention of doing good, but the intention to become manipulators and controllers of the destiny of the world and nations.

Europe had many conflicts and the Rothschild's would finance both sides. What you don't understand is that war is a manipulation of money. You think you're fighting for democracy, a war to end all wars, let peace reign in the earth. This is the tricky language that the wise and the wicked use to trap the poor and the weak. Are you listening?

The House of Rothschild became so strong that even when America was established they kept, through their agents in America, trying to control Central Bank. It hurt to read of the Civil War, people in the South didn't want nobody freeing the slave. I was not evil when I said that "seventy five per cent of Jews owned slaves." I didn't say it. You all wrote it in your own history. But wait, if you owned slaves and they were the bedrock of your wealth you did not want America free. Many were at that root of the confederacy and the Confederate flag yesterday as well as today. Abraham Lincoln was interfering with something bigger than just peace and war.

Rothschild, through his agents in America, financed the North and financed the South, and more lives were lost of poor people who were idealists thinking that they're fighting for these noble principles. And all at the same time you are making the rich richer, but they are enriched at the price of your blood and the blood of your children and the blood of your children's children. See brothers and sisters look, there are many people in the country that know this, but they do not have the voice of the poor. What makes it so dangerous for me to know it and even say it, is because I have the voice and the ear of poor people and once you know the truth it is very difficult for you to go back into your sleep. So naturally to say these things, it puts the spokesperson at great risk.

Because America has been built on your backs, and if any truth comes to remove you, that's like somebody creating an earthquake. You see a beautiful building, but when the earth under it shakes the walls come down, the ceiling comes down. So that's why you've never been allowed a leader that could stay with you to speak to the masses of Black people. Every time you had a leader that could speak to the masses he was cut down, and he's cut down because the country is built on the backs of poor, poor white, poor Black, poor Jews.

Look brothers and sisters in 1922, I'm sorry 1912, on December the 22nd, the Central Bank of America was taken over by certain families. The Federal Reserve that prints the money is not owned by the government. Inside the government betrayal went down and under the presidency of Woodrow Wilson who was elected in 1912, the Federal Reserve system was established in 1913. He came in [in] 1912, Federal Reserve became an Act of law in 1913, and in the same year 1913, IRS was established, FBI was established and the Anti Defamation League of B'nai B'rith was established. And it's not an accident that these four entities were set up in the same year and I'll tell you why.

Now there ain't no use in you getting frightened, because I am doing the talking. So all you can say is "I happened to be there, Lord I am sorry I went," but after you know the truth it's on you. Now all of this is not Revelation, you can find this in your libraries. I want you college students to go and study this, because all your knowledge of economics and finance is worthless, if you don't know the root of this thing. Now listen.

Did you know that at 1912 when Woodrow Wilson was elected, the debt of America was about one billion dollars. When Woodrow Wilson left office by 1920 the debt had risen eight hundred times what it was when he came into office. How did that happen? Now you say "How does that impact on you in 1995?" Can you hold on a few more minutes?

Look brothers and sisters, in 1912, Woodrow Wilson was elected, 1913 IRS is established. Why was the Internal Revenue established? Because those who took control of the money knew that they were going to increase the debt of the country, and they had to have a way to recoup the debt. So the revenue was supposed to be a graduated income tax. This is the way it was put before Congress; which by the way a graduated income tax is the second plank in the Communist manifesto, by Karl Marx.

When you hear the Republicans talking about taking back government and giving it back to the people, it's because the government was moving the country on a socialist trend. Oh, man this thing is deep. Look, Woodrow Wilson comes in and he's going to keep America out of the war. The war started in 1914, is that right? Woodrow Wilson's second term is in 1916, he's keeping America out of the war. This is how they talk when it's time to get elected. But the big boys behind the door, knew that the only way to increase the debt, was to somehow get America involved in the war that was raging in 1914.

So through the manipulation of an incident with a ship called the Lusitania, America declared war on Germany, and in 1917 the American soldiers went to war in Europe. And in order to fight the war America had to borrow money. So who do you borrow money from? From those who print the Treasury bonds. Then they put interest on what America borrows, so the poor people are taxed to pay the interest. Moreover, 1918, Woodrow Wilson leaves office in 1920 and America, that was one billion dollars in debt when he came in is now eight billion dollars in debt, eight hundred times what it was, and the interest the American people are paying.

It was the "war to end all wars," and in that war many of our Black brothers were arguing and fighting because they wanted to fight for America, this great country, not knowing that the whole thing was manipulated by a handful of wicked men, J.P Morgan, the Rockefellers, Loeb and Kuhn, and Schiff, and the Warburg's, and the Rothschilds. These are Anglo-Saxons and Jews, because it does not make any difference when you get to a certain level, we don't see ethnicity, we seek money. Do you understand what I am saying?

Now, World War I is gone. Follow me. Now here we are, Hitler rises. Hitler is trying to get back what was taken from him and the Kaiser and Germany after World War I. Hitler starts moving in Europe and there ain't nobody saying nothing. "Where are you going Hitler?" Hitler sees himself as some kind of messiah. And guess who financed him? You see this is what they do not want to talk about. But Warburg and Rothschilds; these are Jews, and some in America financed Hitler. Warburg a Jew, can travel in Europe at the height of the war, sleep in fine hotels while Jews are being burned in ovens. Now will the real anti-Semite stand up.

A CRIMINAL ORGANISATION

Now look, this is known in certain circles. Many young Jews don't know nothing about this. They are made to see Farrakhan as the enemy, Farrakhan is not your enemy. Your people are using me to get money from you. Oh, I am going to expose them all today. They say that the FBI was set up to catch criminals, well, that's true, but the FBI is a criminal organisation. Oh, Farrakhan how can you say a thing like that in staid old Springfield? It's the best place to say things like this, in staid old Springfield.

The FBI has been a criminal organisation, they don't care nothing about law. They break the law to get at every Black leader, or white leader, anybody who can disrupt, destabilise, excite the poor under the name Communism, under the name of any kind of thing they can think of, they come after you. Listen good now.

You know the FBI's history where we are concerned. Was Mark Clark and Fred Hampton criminals? They were members of the Panther party. Was Marcus Garvey a criminal? Was Noble Drew Ali a criminal? Was W.E.B Du'Bois a criminal? Was Paul Robeson a criminal? Was Martin Luther King a criminal? Well damn it, how could you have streets named from Martin Luther King Junior, and you hypocrites line up on the 16th, and you take ads out in the paper to celebrate the memory of a man that the FBI bugged his hotel, worked against him night and day. Tell me I am lying. They hated Doctor King. What is the real truth of his assassination? They hated Malcolm, and they hated Elijah Muhammad, and they hated the NAACP and the Urban League, and they worked night and day to destabilise every Black organisation. Now tell me I'm a liar.

Let's, let's, let's look a little deeper, just bear with me a few more minutes. If it gets a little bit hot, just fan yourself it'll cool down. Everything's going to be alright. Don't, don't, don't be frightened for me, don't even allow the thought to enter your heart to be frightened for me, you need to be frightened for yourself. Because when they are this wicked and you don't even know it, and I'm going to tell you wars that they contrived and you lost your loved ones, and I lost mine over something which was not any thing at all.

FERMENTING WARS

Let me tell you, World War II jumps up. Hitler was moving in Germany. Do you know what manipulation that was being done economically to strangle Japan? You do not. All you know is that Japan attacked Pearl Harbour. Well they did, they really did. But what would make a little nation like Japan attack a big giant like America? You ain't never thought about that. If you see a flee jump on an elephant you got to ask yourself is the flee crazy or did the elephant excite the flee? When they jumped on America, Franklin Delano Roosevelt, who was considered a great saviour, who introduced the WPA and the CCC, all these social programmes that helped a lot of us out. I ain't lying.

I have to say as a child of welfare that I am grateful for the welfare that my mother received. My father wasn't there for me, but government was. I can't attack that. My mother was an honourable woman, she worked as well as took welfare. And when the welfare lady came to our house, these people come around and look and see what you got. My mom's house was spotless clean and she had nice furniture, and the woman wondered how my mom could live like this on welfare. My mother took the woman in her dining room in a little nook and showed her her power sewing machine, and said "I take in sewing, and I clean all ye floors. I wash all ye pots and I cook all ye food." They used to call me Gene in those days. She said "Gene and Alvin, get you violin get to the piano and play for the lady." Well, when I took my violin and my brother the piano, and I played for the lady, the lady said she understood that my mother wanted to make something of her children.

I graduated high school at sixteen and the day I graduated a cheque came, and my mother took the cheque back to the welfare people, and told them "thank you for getting me this far I think we can take it the rest of the way." I'll deal with welfare reform as we close, but brothers and sisters did you know that we got into World War II on a fluke? And we lost lives and the debt grew because we had to borrow money - right?

After the Second World War was over, Japan was conquered, Germany destroyed, fascism in Italy down. Well what happened? Little did you know, that right out of America and England, Trotsky and Lenin were financed, and Trotsky and Lenin went back to Russia and started the Bolshevik revolution with money from the same international bankers. Now, when the war with Germany and Japan, and Italy was over all of a sudden, the Red Army; communism, became the next threat. This is how the international bankers keep those kings and rulers that they lend money to. Honest, they always have after every war a balance of war in the region and they finance both sides.

Now check this out; the International Bankers financed the Communists. Communists develop some technology, a beautiful new tank that can do this and that. Somebody comes before the Appropriations Committee in Washington, "We need a better tank, well we are going to appropriate so much and so much money." You never asked them "well where is the money coming from?" Then they borrow more and more and more.

Reagan, when Reagan came into office, America was the leading creditor nation and in eight years this man leaves office and America is the leading debtor nation. How did all of that happen? You don't understand. He comes up with "Star Wars." We going out in space, we going to fight it, and the poor American people say "oh, Lord, they've got these rockets, oh, we need some more rockets." So they got rockets, the International Bankers financing the Communists, then we got to get more rockets. They got nuclear weapons, we got to have them. They put a man in space we got to put two, they put four we got to put eight. And where's the money coming from? Where is the money coming from? It ain't got nothing to do with welfare.

Your little stuff that you get is a piddling compared to what government has wasted of the tax payers money in weapons of war, trillions of dollars spent on weapons. And after the Soviet Union collapsed, the first thing they talk about is "well let's go and destroy, you know nuclear weapons, there's a proliferation." Now all the money that you put into all these big bombs - your money. You living under a bridge - your money. You're eating dog food - your money that they been taking from you ever since you worked, in social security.

Now they're eating away your social security benefits. Going on about don't touch social security, they've already raped her. Like Malcolm said "she being took, she being had, she being bamboozled." They got your money and gone and they're betting that you are not going to even live to collect social security, because now they're talking about raising the age limit to seventy years. Boy this thing is tricknology.

Now we out of World War II, in more debt. Communism up, more debt. China coming now. "Oh Lord, a billion of them over there and they got an atomic weapon." Oh man. More and more weapons in America, more and more tax payers money eaten up, mean while the roads are corroding, the bridges are falling down, the schools are not getting adequate care. I mean look at your country, look at yourself.

Well the communists are moving in Asia, "Oh my God, they're taking over South-East Asia you guys." The French got whipped in Vietnam and a ding pin few, just a few got out alive. Now America says "let's get in, let's get in." Jack Kennedy is in office. Jack Kennedy wants to come out of Vietnam. Jack Kennedy talking about printing money. Jack Kennedy dead.

If he comes out of Vietnam the bankers do not get the money. "Come on boys, Uncle Sam wants you, come on boys Communism is taking over the world boys," and the same bankers financed it, keep it going. But you now got to die. Poor whites, poor Blacks, poor Jews, poor Gentiles, poor Native Americans, come on to Korea, come on to Vietnam. Oh they'll give you a purple heart, they will even drape a flag over your dead body. Fire a twenty-one gun salute and tell you how grateful [the] nation [is], and all [the] time you died for nothing. You died to enrich the wickedly wise, bloodsuckers of the poor.

This is why they fear truth. I mean it makes you angry does it not? Think about your uncles, think about your fathers, think about your cousins, think about your people white and Black who died thinking that they were fighting for democracy. Look, that ain't the half of it. Lyndon Johnson tricked the American people into the war in Vietnam on another lie, on what is called the Tunkin Gulf Resolution. We were in the war, Jack Kennedy trying to get us out, they're not going to have that, he is popped. Now, LBJ is his Vice president, but he is cool because he's our man because he is going to increase and widen the war. Look at the thing.

So he steps in, and it is no accident. He steps in and the Tunkin Gulf Resolution, which is a trick. "Westy West Morgan we can not let him down." Five hundred thousand American troops sent to Vietnam. Do you know how much money it takes to move five hundred thousand troops, to move nine thousand miles away? Do you know how much ordinance, weapons, ammunition has to be there? How much business is cranked up just at the thought of supporting five hundred thousand of our fighting men? How much factories waxed rich developing aeroplanes and tanks to fight in Vietnam? And do you know that when the Viet-Kong came down on Saigon, they left billions of dollars in equipment, and gold, and money behind running for their lives? And some of our family came back dope addicts because they were never trained to fight people like the Viet-Kong.

People lived underground, just crawled into a hole, and got little works almost like little towns under the ground. You bombing them and bombing them and you swear that they got to be dead, and they crawl up out the ground and tear your backside up. They booby-trapped, I mean you can not imagine the hell and the horror that your children went through in Vietnam, and because the American public getting more and more enlightened stood against the war.

ASSASSINATIONS

And here comes our brother Martin Luther King Junior. As long as Martin Luther King Junior was trying to integrate a toilet, or a coffee stand or a hotel or a motel he was a good nigger. "Oh yes, that Martin Luther King Junior is just a wonderful man. What is he saying now, that we should come out of Vietnam? Wait, he's meddling, niggers are not supposed to talk about international affairs - stick to the Negro stuff, don't dabble into international affairs and geopolitics."

The FBI went to work. The FBI tried to get the Pope not to recognise him, tried to get the Nobel Peace Commission not to give him the medal. They bugged his hotel and sent a tape of what they bugged to his wife. These are the bastards that say they are for democracy, these are the illegitimate reptiles of American society. It's alright for you to have a King holiday today, because there is no more King. You don't even know what the hell Doctor King stood for; "I have a dream," when the hell did he have a dream and when did he wake up to reality?

They killed him because he was interfering with the war. Big business, big money. He's dead, Bobby is dead, Jack is dead. Anybody that interferes with their global ambition, but I'll be damned if you going to kill me. By the help of Almighty God, I am going to be your worst nightmare. By the help of Almighty God I have a backer today. My brothers didn't make it through, but I'm going to make it, if it pleases Allah, and we are going to make it.

And now, and now Martin is gone, Malcolm is gone, these wicked people manipulated the circumstances inside the Nation. They manipulated envy and jealousy inside the Nation against Malcolm X. They manipulated us, so when Malcolm split from The Honourable Elijah Muhammad we in the Nation who loved Elijah Muhammad and loved Malcolm had to choose. I was one of those who was taught and reared by Malcolm like a father. I was his student. I adored him but not more than The Honourable Elijah Muhammad. I adored him because he was the greatest representative of the man I loved. So when he split from the man I loved, I was put in the position that children are put in when parents divorce.

You don't understand the pain of your children. You don't know what it means to have children see the people who brought them into existence, destroying each other. You don't know what that means for a child to be in the custody of a mother that is constantly berating and talking down the father, and when the father has visitation rights with the child the father is talking down on the mother, the child is confused.

They manipulated us. I fought for The Honourable Elijah Muhammad. That meant that I fought against Malcolm my brother, my teacher. I don't regret standing up for The Honourable Elijah Muhammad, but I regret that we were used to create the atmosphere, that allowed Malcolm to be killed and Elijah Muhammad and the Nation get the blame. Well where the hell is the government in all of this? This didn't happen in a vacuum. Go read the files of the US government. Go read what the FBI did.

Malcolm wanted protection after his house was firebombed. How come he went to the Audobaun ball-room and there was no uniformed policeman, nowhere in sight? How come a man who had always searched the people on that day decided he was not going to search? How come two men were arrested at the scene and only one stood trial, and there never was a mention of who that second man was? How come two other men went to prison for twenty six years of their lives for a crime they had nothing to do with? And the very man who was involved, exonerated them. Kuntsler had the names of all those who were involved and went to the government to re-open the case and the government refused to reopen the case.

This is the same government; FBI, that paid an informant $45,000 to entrap Malcolm's daughter. A young Jew who said "He's an enemy of the Jews and an enemy of your father," working on that child then paying money, but that's only the tip of the iceberg. You know the government wasn't going to let Michael Fitzpatrick or Michael Sumers kill me. Why if a Jew killed me, what the hell do you think is going to happen in this country?

Do you think that you taught us how to kill in World War 1, II, Vietnam and Korea and don't have nothing for us and then would kill the very people that speak to our hurt, and we will not go crazy? They don't want no white person to kill me. They wanted me to react to Quibillah, in the way I reacted to her father. They wanted to recreate the same atmosphere again. To put nationalists against Muslims, and orthodox Muslims against followers of Elijah Muhammad. There's already money out there to do the job, by that same government.

NEW WORLD ORDER

"Soviet Union is gone now, well what other war can we create? Let's see, we got to keep this debt going up." But bankers don't you have a heart? I mean the country is $4 trillion in debt, to service that debt is nearly $350 billion a year, you only take in $1 trillion in taxes, over one third of it is paying interest on a debt. So if Clinton who put a budget before Congress of one trillion, six hundred billion ($1,600 billion), which means that if he cuts taxes, lord you all have got to understand this language man, they talking about cutting taxes and they only get a trillion in taxes. If they cut taxes, now they raise the budget from $1.5 to $1.6 billion, then there is $1 trillion, six hundred billion. So you got $600 billion more than you taking in, in taxes. So you got to borrow money just to see your budget through. So by the time this man lcaves office the debt may be $6 trillion. Which means that whatever you take in, in taxes, has to go to service the debt, so America then is bankrupt.

Now the people who want a one world order, look at Bush's crazy self. These are your leaders and they ain't worth a damn, none of them. They have sold the American people out. You don't even, are not even considered in this Blackman and woman. You are the biggest pawn in the game, you not even considered. They don't even consider selling you out, because you were nothing to begin with, in their eyes. I know it hurts. I know it hurts.

Look man, Bush talking about a New World Order. What is a New World Order? It started with the League of Nations, then it escalated to the United Nations. Now it is a New World Order, and in a New World Order power has to be taken from every nation of power, so that they will bow down to a new power. You don't hear me. America is being stripped of power, the sex revolution, you all got your head in your pants and these people are taking the world over while you are looking at your genitals. Are you listening to me? I'm not being vulgar. I am telling you what is happening to your world.

Your children are shaking their backsides, at two years old they can shake. Roll it tootsie. It's all fun to you and while your tootsies' rolling, they rolling you up and getting you ready for the slaughter. You young white people with your head full of dope and damn guitar and your long hair. Your whole country going to hell and you got long hair and you don't even know whether you're a man or woman. An earring in your damn ear, one in your nose and you are all sexed up.

Not to think of you Black brother, I don't know what the hell your problem is? You just as crazy as you could be. Sisters I see you just naked, well you might as well just be naked. If you sneeze you're uncovered, got your dresses up so high and some of you are grandmothers. Who the hell want to look at your thighs? Grandma trying to snatch her somebody, ought to be ashamed of yourself, all that cellulite, stretch marks and broken veins. Cover your damn self now if you got sense, you should be a woman of dignity ruling from your wisdom and not from your body.

We all gone crazy. I can't turn the radio on, turn the television on, I see my sister with her backside in the television almost butt naked, just shaking and bumping and grinding and the whole damn world going to hell. I mean look how stupid you look. They have programmed you for self destruction and now you running around with your hat turned funny. One colour on another colour and you got the wrong sign, so we shoot this brother down, kill this one, guns all in your neighbourhood. When the hell did a white man ever want to see a Blackman with a gun? And why do you think the guns are there? I know you think you have some weaponry, you crazy as hell. They have set you up for the slaughter, the whole world has been made ready. They see the fall of America and they are blaming it on you, when the real fault is these wicked international bankers who have manipulated government, religion, education, science, but you are the scapegoat.

And so my dear family, Iran arose with Imam Khomenei. You don't know nothing about Khomenei. Khomenei is a sincere religious man, but he was a no nonsense religious man, a real Muslim. You would call him today a fundamentalist Muslim, meaning he wants to root his life in the fundamentals of Islam. Some are called fundamentalist Christian, which means that they're not deviating from the fundamental basic teachings of Jesus Christ. Nothing wrong with fundamentals, that is what every thing is based on, the fundamentals. Khomenei came to power after America caused the destruction of Muhammad Musadec who was a Muslim who wanted to control the oil of Iran and draw the benefit of that oil for the Iranian people. The CIA caused him to be overthrown and the Shah was sat on the throne in Iran. In Indonesia the CIA caused over five hundred thousand peoples' lives to be lost.

The CIA involved in the destruction of Patrice Lamunmba. CIA tried to kill Michael Manley of Jamaica and tried to assassinate Fidel Castro and was successful in getting rid of Bishop in Grenada. You don't know the wickedness of your government, I am not anti-government, I am anti the wickedness of government that masquerades as righteous men looking out for the American people, while they are sentencing you to death.

The food merchants have become merchants of death. The tobacco industry knows that they are killing you, but you cannot stop smoking now, "It's a habit now, I've got to have it." Alcohol. Who are the families that control the alcohol? How did the Kennedy family become rich? Who is Myer Lanski and Dutch Schultz? Who are the Jews that are behind the crime and the drugs, as well as Anglo-Saxons? Talk to me damn it.

The Bible don't tell you Jews to be drunkards. So why the hell you create the damn liqueur? And there ain't one Rabbi pointing out these liqueur barons. Where is the righteousness of you? Why don't you stand up for the law that God gave you through Moses? Why don't you say to David Geffin in Hollywood and these corrupt, Hugh Heffner and playboy and hustler magazine. These are your brothers? Why don't you righteous Jews speak out and condemn them, like you want every Blackman to condemn me?

You can't get a dollar from a Jewish organisation until you stand up and condemn Louis Farrakhan. They have made me the litmus test, so some Black person says "Oh Farrakhan ain't no good," he's alright. But I never hear one of them condemn any of the wicked of their own people, but you run your mouth and I have never done one thing against Black people, not one thing. And to make it even worse they call us a hate group, but you can't point to one thing we have ever done to any member of the Jewish community.

You will never find any of us painting on your synagogue, we will defend the synagogue. Any house where God's house is remembered it is our duty to defend. You will never find us overturning tomb stones in a Jewish cemetery. You will never find us attacking members of the Jewish community, but if I tell the truth, now they call me a new Hitler, for exposing the ADL as a gangster organisation. I am not talking about the little Jews, I'm talking about them big ones at the top. Their duty is to protect the international bankers, that's why they were set up. And the moment I mention the international bankers in my Saviours Day address, the ADL took out a full page Ad in the "New York Times" condemning me as an anti-Semite, but they never said that what I said was a lie.

Who is Paul, Max, and Felix Warburg? They don't want to meet me face up in no argument. You can't win in no argument with me, not as long as I stay on the principles of truth, you can't win with me. So you go behind my back, go to college presidents and tell them "Don't allow these Nation of Islam speakers come on the campus." What are you afraid of? I thought you had taught the people truth, well if you made your students so wise, what are you afraid of Nation of Islam Ministers coming there for?

Your education is the biggest trick of all, because they give you a doctorate degree, that you pay for, and a Masters degree that you pay for, and a B.S degree that you pay for, and you can't use nothing that you got to solve the problems of your community. That is worse than a used car salesman selling you a car and keeping the key and all you can do is sit in it, and talk about how sweet it looks, but you can't go no where in it.

So guess what, the evil Empire of Russia has gone. The British Empire that said the sun never set on it, the sun cannot hardly find it today. So all Europe is trying to band together now. Poor Africa, Africa's gone. I know brothers, I love Africa too, I love to hear the drum beat, I like to see the dance, I like to feel the rhythm of Africa, but what am I feeling? You see I'm not a romanticist baby. Africa is nearly $450 billion in debt to who? The IMF and the World Bank and anytime you are in debt you give up some of your sovereignty, and you give up a measure of your own natural resources to pay back the debt. So Europe is more firmly entrenched and in control in Africa today as they ever were. In fact they are more in control.

DESERT STORM

Do you hear me? Alright, so what are we going to do about it, what are we going to do about it? That's where we are going to close, so let us get together and just see what we can do. First I want to say, Iran and Iraq two Muslim countries went to war with each other. Saudi Arabia and the Gulf States, sheikhdoms and the kingdoms set up by the power of the British. They do all these things to create mischief. Kuwait is in fact the nineteenth province of Iraq, did you know that? It's really true. But the British when they set up the sheikhdoms they take some from this, knowing that later there's going to be a border dispute, then the bankers come and finance both sides again. That's why there's all these border wars in Africa. The boys have fixed it. Do you hear me?

The sheikhdoms and Saudi Arabia were so frightened by the rhetoric of Imam Khomenei. America sitting in the back sending Saddam Hussein money. Saddam Hussein has become the big military power in that area of the world, did you know that? Saudi Arabia gave them over $50 billion in their war against Iran, then when the war came to a stale-mate, Iran as a military power was just about destroyed. But Iraq still had juice and America didn't want Iraq strong with Israel there. Iraq built an atomic plant and the moment it was built; the French built it for them at the cost of billions of dollars, the moment it was built Israel bombed it. All that money gone down the drain and the world didn't say nothing. This is some deep stuff.

America and Russia selling the Black world arms, everybody buying guns and they give you the worst in their stock pile.

The high tech weapons they don't give you that, that's why there's weapons in the Black community. Some of those weapons you shoot here and the bullet goes there, they've given you crazy guns. You drive by shooting and think, you think you're shooting at your brother over here and you killed a baby over there. You say "How did that happen? I aimed over here." They give you the worst in the stock pile, stuff that has defects in it but you don't know the defects because you are not an arms merchant. But the arms merchant are waxing rich all over the world selling third world nations antiquated weapons that you can kill each other with. For you sure ain't going to kill them with those antiquated weapons.

America has got high-tech stuff. Iraq felt they were ready now. The American Ambassador told the Iraqi government that was having a problem with Kuwait, that it wouldn't be a problem. So Saddam Hussein moves his troops into Kuwait. Margaret Thatcher leaves England meets with Bush in Denver, and then in the next few days he said "I told Saddam, Saddam has to get out of Kuwait."

But you told Saddam he could go in. Now Saddam is in, Saddam does not want to get out. Now check this out. He gets the whole United Nations to back him. I was in Baghdad, three days before the bombs fell, I'm in Baghdad. What in the world am I doing in Baghdad? They invited me to a conference of revolutionary mullahs, revolutionary they called them, oh I can't think of the name of the Islamic scholars. And I'm sitting there; and I know that this is rough and they want me to speak, and I'm telling you the truth I'm really a little nervous and I don't want to talk because I'm not in agreement with the madness that I'm hearing.

And finally my son-in-law convinced me that you got to say something. Well, I said it. I said look, I meant to give it para-phrase I said "My brothers are down in the desert, Black Christians, that's my family, they're in the desert poised to fight you." I said "They didn't join the army to fight you, they joined the army because there were no jobs available, so the army was a way out of unemployment and they didn't have to get involved in crime. And so now, here they are in the desert, and here you are my Muslim Brothers poised for war against my Christian Brothers."

And then I railed on them and told them that "Your problem ain't Israel, your problem isn't America, your problem is your deviation from the principles of the Qur'an laid down by Prophet Muhammad, (PBUH)." As God is my witness now, I am in their house, but don't ever ask me to speak if you don't want to hear the truth. I really don't care nothing about who you are because there is no king, there is no ruler, there is no potentate more powerful than God. So if you want the truth, then call me and I'll tell it.

They were talking about Holy War. I said "Holy War is not for Saddam, Holy War is for Allah." I said "You can't use Allah when you've got a political problem, now you become a Muslim and when that problem is over we never hear you say Allah-u-Akbar." They talked about the man in Kuwait as having a hundred and forty wives. I said "That may be pretty bad, but what is worse, a man having one hundred and forty wives or you starting a war with another Muslim nation causing a million young Muslims to be killed. Which one's the real hypocrite?" I said it, I said they are poised and Bush is not going to back down. I said "Now if you empower me, I will go back to America and have a conference with Bush and tell him that you as Muslim scholars have decided that this war should stop, and you as Muslims should use the Qur'an to settle the differences between two Muslim nations."

Well you know the international bankers are not going to hear that. Hey listen, do you know Saudi Arabia for the first time had to borrow money after that war? Do you know who benefited from the war? America said in Congress "We came out of this one with a plus." Do you know what happened? They set all the oil fields on fire in Kuwait. Who could put it out? Here comes Jim Dandy to the rescue and the Kuwaitis had almost $250 billion in American banks and it took almost $190 billion to re-build Kuwait.

So America wondered all the way around. Now Saddam is under such constraints, that he's no longer the military power he once was, so Israel can't be threatened so much by Iraq, nor so much by Iran. And America has a presence in Saudi now, that she never had before, and I mean everything seemed to be working in her favour. Yeah! Now let us conclude this.

Look brothers and sisters this thing is so serious that America really, really, really is being undermined, not by Louis Farrakhan but by those who want to weaken America so much that you'll find revolution in the streets. And I'm saying this, if they cut out any support to the poor the poor are going to revolt, and I'm not talking about poor Black people. The whites of this nation are exceedingly angry and they are more and more dissatisfied than you have ever seen white people in a long, long time, with government and with politics. That's why they're not voting anymore because they don't care about this anymore and they are angry as hell because they see the country being taken from them. And they are armed, and dangerous, and while they are planning to kill you, something else is going on inside the house. Now, how do we get out of this?

SOLUTIONS IN A DECLINE

The Bible says, in my conclusion, I know you can't wait for me to get there, but I don't want you to leave me. I want you to hear the whole thing. The Bible says "come out of her my people that you be not partakers of her sins and her plagues, for her sins have reached unto heaven." Then another place it says "Babylon is fallen, is fallen she has become a habitation of devils and a hole of every foul spirit and a cage for every unclean and hateful bird." This is not talking about ancient

Babylon, it's talking about a mystery Babylon. A Babylon that would be at the end of the world that looked like a golden chalice on the outside but filth and abomination on the inside. That's America, a habitation of devils and a hole of every foul spirit and a cage for every unclean and hateful bird.

The unclean birds are the birds of prey and right now America has become a place where everybody is preying on, not praying for, preying on somebody else. Look at it, you take your car to the mechanic he preys on you, you go to a lawyer for a simple case he preys on you, you go to a doctor and he prescribes medicine and the druggist charges you year-long bills for something that they know does not cost that much. The druggist is preying on you, the doctor is preying on you, you go to church where somebody should be praying for you and the preacher is preying on you, you go to school - I mean look at you. You walk the streets at night or drive, and come up to a stop and your brother puts a gun in your face and says "Get out the car," he takes your car and shoots you down, rapes your daughter.

This is America, a habitation of devils and a hole of every foul spirit and a cage for every unclean and hateful bird. But she's fallen, she's fallen and she will take you down with her, if you don't come out of her. How do I come out of her? How do I come out? Is it that I must run to Africa? There's no hiding place.

Here is how you come out. You come out spiritually and mentally from the bondage of being wrapped up in a world that's sucking you down into its fall, you come out mentally, morally and spiritually. But now you've got to extricate yourself economically. "Well how can I do it Farrakhan, how can I do it?" This paper money called the Federal Reserve note that used to be a Silver Certificate, that used to have on it "Pay to the bearer on demand a dollar in silver or the equal in silver," that ain't on there no more, because you can't get real money for this money that you got in your pocket. The only thing that you can do with that money is trade that money for goods and services. Now, while it has some value we got to pool as much of it as we can. What should we buy? We should buy earth, earth that does not loose its value when the currency is inflated or deflated, the land will always be able to feed you with sunshine, water and seeds.

Look, you going to have to come now and do something for yourself. You got clothes but we don't make them, you got shoes but we don't make them, you got homes but we don't build them. Now if we took the money that we throw away and began to rebuild, first we would take ourselves off of government as a burden and begin to use what we extract from this nation to build up our own selves and our own community.

Look, if you will walk with me I want a million Black men, listen, listen, listen. I want a million Black men not to read history or to be on the sideline of history, but I want a million Black men to make history with me. If a million Black men show up in Washington, what is your purpose? First we want to call for a Day of Atonement.

"What do you mean a Day of Atonement?" We as Black men have to atone for the evils that we have permitted to destroy our own communities and our own families, particularly our women. We as Black men have to atone for our slothfulness in putting our woman out front and letting her suffer the slings and the arrows and the abuse of this world to help her man make advancement while many of us stayed on the sidelines or stayed at home. We as Black men have to atone for making children and allowing government to support the issue of our lives. We have to atone for selling drugs and dealing death in our communities, sending these women to funeral parlours and graveyards burying their children because of our madness or our lack of strength as men to stand up against the madness that's going on in our own communities.

A Day of Atonement, and last but not least, a Day of Atonement for failure to take up our responsibility as men to become the providers for our families and the leaders of our own communities. We have to atone for that. See, God is choosing you today, us today. With all due respect to the Jewish people you have been chosen, but you failed in your commitment. Now God chose another and the book says "He would choose the despised and the rejected, He would choose the bottom rail and bring it to the top. Thou shall no more be the tail but the head." Who is the tail? Who is the bottom? Who is the least? Who is the foolish? It is we, God has chosen us.

But Blackman you can't accept your role from God until you come in sackcloth and ashes and atone and repent for your and my slothfulness and wickedness. And if a million of us show up in Washington, we not drugged, we not going there unintelligent. We're in ranks like a solid wall proclaiming our liberation and our willingness to take up our responsibility as free men and then we going to call on America to atone for her wickedness, for her evils done. You got to make America know her rottenness and I don't think that there is anybody that can make her know it better.

Make her to know her sins and then call on America. "You got to atone." What do you mean atone? You just don't repent and say I'm sorry, but you got to do something. Here, we are the representatives of forty million people. We are saying to America "alright, you don't have a lot of money we understand the constraints that you are under, but you got a whole lot of land out here that you are not doing nothing with. It's going to take about fifty million acres just to feed forty million people and clothe them. Since you got government land that you ain't doing nothing with, then I want you to lease it to us, sell it to us or down right give it to us for what we have done to build your country and to defend freedom we have never enjoyed." We want reparations, you got to do something to repair the damage that four hundred years of injustice has done.

But whether they do anything or not we got to take the responsibility. With $400 billion coming through our hands every year, if we can just attract 10% of that back into our own communities, $40 billion we can start building our own community and an economy that will cause us to survive. So whether government does anything or not it is irrelevant, immaterial and baseless. We got to do it for ourselves. A million Black men. Look at the political drama. A million Black men on a Monday, on a Monday, not on a Saturday and not on a Sunday, but on a Monday, which is supposed to be a work day. On October 16, mark it down on your calendar. I don't know whether you have ever seen the play, I never saw it but I heard about it, called "The Day of Absence."

I want us to think about that, because on that day we're not going to work. "What you say Farrakhan?" I'm going to say it again, on that day we're not going to work, we're going to Washington. We're going to do a different work. On that day the children don't go to school, "what! as ignorant as we are?" No, on that day, Black woman you don't go to the office, you don't go down town, you don't hit no damn typewriter, you don't do nothing down town. On that day, every Black woman gather your children in your homes and start to get again acquainted with your responsibility and your role as a mother, and a shaper of the destiny of your people. On that day while we are in Washington, you're at home with your children, in a day of prayer, and a day of teaching your children the value of unity. When they turn on the television and see a million or more, tell them what unity will do what a gun will could never do. Unity will do what armies can't do. In unity the children of Israel marched around the walls of Jericho and shouted in unison, and brought the walls down. There was not a gun in sight.

You stay home. If you are going to do some shopping, shop the Saturday before, but on that Monday they don't even see you in Bloomingdales, they don't see you at J.C. Penny's, Carson Puree-Scot, they don't see you in Fileens basement, they don't see you in none of the fine shoe stores and boutiques, because on that day it's a day of absence. I want white folk to see what America going to look like when there's no Black folk in sight. You say you don't want us, I want to show you something.

On that day, ain't going to be no Blackman hitting no baseball, ain't going to be no Blackman dunking any baseball, ain't going to be no Blackman running no football. We're going to let it be all white that day because all white on that day is alright on that day. Let us see what football look like with no Black folk running the ball. What does basket-ball look like with no Black folk playing the game? What does baseball look like with no Black folk hitting the ball?

We're going to take the colour out of America, we're going to take the salt out of the food. We won't play no blues that day. We won't play no trumpet that day. We won't blow no horn that day. We won't do no rap that day. We don't entertain for nobody that day. It's a Day of Atonement.

And while you are doing that in the home, those brothers that can't make it to Washington, you got to do something to show that you're in sympathy with us. You go to your families, it's a Day of Atonement. You got to go and tell your wife "I'm sorry." You got to tell each other "I'm sorry, forgive me for what I did wrong, can you forgive me, can you allow me to atone for what I haven't done or what I did wrong." You make up with your estranged wife so that even if you can't be her husband, you're her brother. If she can't be your wife, she's your sister, in faith, in God, and you got to make it right for the children's sake.

Then you got to go to your children whom you messed over, the lighter one whom you pushed up and the darker one whom you pushed down, and you've got to make a Day of Atonement and say "I am sorry, I did not know any better and that is why I did not do any better, but from this day forward," and then all over America a change will start taking place. We don't have to go to the government and declare a holiday or ask government to vote on one, we going to declare our own holiday and make it real. Do you hear me Black Brother and Sister?

But that's not all, a million men is an army, but what kind of army? You used to sing it in the church "Onward Christian soldiers," but you don't know what a Christian soldier is if you still in the church, you got to come out of the church and march on Satan, march on his world as a righteous emissary of God and His Christ. We got to do it, we got to do it. Now what happens beyond?

Every brother that comes, he has to register to vote. You said "for what Farrakhan?" Just hold on a minute. I'm goner ask those who wish to come out of the Democratic party I don't think they have treated us right. I am goner ask those in the Republican party, come out of the party and re-register as an independent. Here's why. In 1996 a Presidential election is coming up. We know they ain't the real government, but we can extract from it some benefit if we hold our vote solid.

AN AGENDA
FOR THE PEOPLE

We're going to develop an agenda for our people, it's not going to be Muslim developing it, it's goner be all of us developing an agenda. After the "Million Man March" we do town-hall meetings throughout this country talking to Black people, getting the pulse of our people and making an agenda for us. And then in 1996 when it is election time the same way they go to the synagogue and put on a yamak and tell members of the Jewish community what they do for Israel and what they goner do here, and what they goner do there, we goner make them put on a dashiki and say Oh, or wrap themselves in some Kente cloth and come in front of us, and tell us how you - what you feel about our agenda here.

We'll already have legislation already prepared to go through Congress that deals with the plight of our people. We're not going to allow them to put you in jail for the rest of your life when the whole society has been geared towards you simply because they say, "three strikes." Hell no, that's a modern slave plantation that they're preparing for the Blackman and we're not going to let it go down.

Now if you don't think that our unity is power, I really want to show you something if you back me up. There ain't goner be no more going to war, they got to come by us first. Well what you mean war? "Well we have just declared war," we don't give a damn who you declared it on; well let me tell you, wait, wait, wait, wait man let me tell you something. I know you scared as hell, I know that, but dog-it - but a scared to-death Negro ain't worth a damn. Do you hear me? Do you want to be free? But a scared Negro is never goner be free.

When Jesus came to Peter walking on the water; hell I would be shook-up if I seen a man walking on water, the man was walking on water. Jesus said come on Peter "step out of the boat." That's heavy brother. See the boat is built under the law of buoyancy. You in the boat and you look pretty good unless the rain and the winds capsize the boat, but to tell you "Come out of the boat" and start walking like your Master on the water, hey that takes some faith. And Peter got out and he started walking, and he said "oh wee," and he took his eyes off the master and he went to sinking, and the Master up-held him. But the lesson is a lesson of faith. See God is with us to do what is right, and if you exercise some faith in God; and when I say exercise faith in God, stand still when you don't know where you are going.

You say "Well there's a war," well wait a minute, let us talk about this war, "but we have the right we're the President of the United States, we sent you greetings." And we sent them back! You don't greet us no more. And I guarantee you, you stand up, they'll back up. Here some sissies standing up,

"Now darling," and you know if they can stand and force the government to back up, don't tell, don't ask and you all can be in the army, the navy, anything you all want to be in. Well what backed them up? Five hundred thousand gays marched in Washington. That sent a message to all politicians and they scared to offend gay people.

Well one million Black men representing ten million more, hell I want to terrify them to do anything to upset us. Now when they get ready to go to war they got to think now. And you that are Hispanic if you ain't got a leader to talk for you, don't worry I'll speak. You Native Americans if you ain't got nobody to talk for you don't worry about it, I'll talk for you. You poor white folk I'll talk for you too, I'll have a little harder time, but I'll talk for you.

You stand with me and I say to the government of America, wait a minute, "Let's go back into this, how did you get into this war? because poor people are going to die." I'm not goner be the one to die because I'm too old according to their standards. I'm too old to be drafted and my mother always told me "Don't get in no draft - you'll catch a cold." But we not goner let them use you no more. That's the point.

If America is sincerely in trouble, well we got to defend where we live if she is in trouble, but don't manufacture trouble just to make some money for the greedy and poor people to die. We're not going for that no more. Now you know they don't want me to live, that's common sense, hey, you know they upset. Tell them die in their rage because we goner get stronger everyday. So to our sisters, to our sisters, when we make this march we want our women to be solidly behind your men.

For all these years you've been out front and you've been the wind beneath our wings. We wouldn't be where we are if it were not for our women. You have been patient with us while we have been a mess and now we're asking you to let us show you our appreciation and our love for you, and our gratitude

to you by taking the point for where we should have been all
these years. And when we go to Washington from all over this
nation in unity, Christians, Muslims, Nationalists, Baptists,
people of no religion, oh what a day. No song will be sung
that day that has anything to do with anything else but spiritual
values, no rap, nothing, I am talking about at the march, and
the speeches will be speeches that have wisdom and guidance
for Black men. And after that we intend to stay together and
put pressure on ourselves and on corporate America.

She gives too little and gets too much. How many of you own
automobiles, would you raise your hand? That's a lot of cars.
How many of you own a General Motors product, would you
raise your hand? How many of you own a Ford product? How
many of you own a Chrysler product? How many of you own a
Japanese made product? Okay, now what are they doing for us
for the billions of dollars that they take out of our community?

Suppose we represent you now and we go to GM. "Mr
Motors, last year you took out of the Black community 'X'
amount of billions of dollars. What we want is a partnership
with you and a plant set up in the Black community. We'll
determine how many plants and sit and talk with you." Listen
now, listen this is not pipe dream talk, you just don't know
what your unity can produce because you ain't never tried it.
You never tried it.

But when you look at what they get from you, and all you get
is a commercial with Michael Jordan in a Chevrolet, or Mikey
with Nike. What did you get out of that? Well now you the
one buying the Nike's, they're using Michael and your love of
Michael to sell Nikey. That ain't goner work no more, Mike
has got his but the Black community they don't have nothing.
That's not going to work no more. So look man, you sending
these factories; you making them in third world countries, the
Black communities, the inner cities is like third world. So
what we going to leverage is; you going to give us 'X'
amount, and we goner to be partners. We're not coming to

work we own it with you. Well what are we putting in? Sweat, equity, and all the billions we've being putting in should have got us something in here.

Now look at this, if they don't do this, then we don't buy no more General Motors. Don't buy it no more. Have you ever seen what your money could do when you stop. See that's where white folk, you know, you know they talk to you then because you hit them where it hurts, and I mean hit them. Then after you do that to General Motors we go to Ford, then we go to Mitsubishi, Sony, whoever. Then let's come back and deal with Pepsi, then Coca-Cola. Deal with corporate America and make them respond to the needs of a people whose blood they are sucking.

Do you hear me? Now you can give whatever you want to give Michael, but that ain't helping the little people that don't have a job. You goner put a Nike factory in several cities and in the mean time back at the ranch, we are going to be pooling our resources to build for ourselves, and in the next ten to fifteen years under that kind of leadership you'll see yourself elevated to the level of respect all over the world.

In fact if you march with me to Washington I guarantee you America will never be the same again and all over this earth they'll take another look at Black people. You say "Well, what about you, will this make you the pre-eminent leader?" Well you can get personal, you can get personal, but if a million people answer the call it's because they know something about the brother. Don't let envy get in the way here, because I am not a fool. I know I am going to die sooner or later I am out of here. So while God has given me this moment in time, don't be no fool.

Support me and let me do what God has put in my heart to do, so that when I am no longer here to do, a foundation will be laid for your son and your grandson, and your daughter and your granddaughter, because it is not about no personalities. We as personalities live and we die.

In closing, somebody said "Farrakhan, I saw all those people lined up coming up to see you, how does that make you feel?" I said "Brother that don't make me feel no different than I did thirty years ago when I sat in your office to have you put some braces on my teeth." I said "There were generations before where there were persons that people lined up to see, that person is dead and the people that lined up to see him are dead and generations have come and generations have gone, but God was, God is, and God shall always be."

So none of us who are born into this world to serve you are worthy of worship, only God should be worshiped. We are a passing reality, but God is forever. So when you fasten your heart on God and not on these personalities that come and go, and if you can see in us while we are alive value, because God is using us as an instrument for that time for a specific purpose, then give God the glory and then help that person. See you didn't help Martin Luther King, that's why you have all these holidays because you didn't do right by him. You never did right by Malcolm, you lie if you say you did.

You never did right by Garvey or none of the great ones because you were too frightened. But now you got a chance, were going to Washington and beyond. All the brothers here tonight how many of you would like to stand with Brother Farrakhan and let's stand for our people, may I see your hands?

Would you stand up Blackman? How many of you want to go with me to Washington? Let me see your hands? Would you stand up brothers? Look at them sisters. Those of you who can't make it that day, how many of you will be in sympathy and support for us that day? Would you just let us see your hand. I am talking about men now, men, men, just men.

Now sisters, how many sisters will be in support of your brothers if they march with us that day? How many women will stand in support of your man? You will? Well here is what I want you to do. Every brother that said you are going to march, go and get ten, get ten more like yourself and say "Come on man were going." And sisters those of you who goner back us you go get ten sisters so that by the time October come, all of Black America, all of Hispanic America, all of Native American-America will be on fire. And then we will send a message to the government and a message to the world.

May God bless each of you and if you would like to get your instructions on the march you can call 1900-97-MARCH. Thank you for staying with me this long, thank you for your time, thank you for your attention, may Allah bless you all as I greet you in peace

As-Salaam-Alaikum.